Birgitte Krag Hansen

NEW FELT
using the felting needle

Klematis✳

New Felt
First published in Denmark
i 2003 by © Forlaget Klematis A/S
Original title: Ny filt med filtenålen

Text and illustration copyright: © Birgitte Krag Hansen, 2004
Photo copyright: © Claus Dalby
Editor: Claus Dalby
Layout: Marianne Schultz
English translation: Ian Lukins
© 2004 Forlaget Klematis A/S
www.klematis.dk
Printed by Abildgaard Grafisk A/S Aalborg, Denmark

ISBN 87-7905-877-9

Contents

Introduction

The craft of felting has in many ways had its technique revolutionised with the introduction of the felting needle, because this needle can bind the wool together simply by being pushed into the wool.

The processes that earlier demanded much greater amounts of time, water, and patience have now become a lot easier and quicker to handle; as well as giving sheer joy and pleasure from completely new, amazing possibilities.

I have used the felting needle for five years, since I was told about it by one of my American e-mail contacts, and it has been an indispensable tool ever since.

The needle does not look very impressive on sight, but it is fantastic what this comparatively simple tool can do with wool. It has very sharp barbs that can pull wool fibres down into the underlying material and thus felt it.

It is surprising to think how long it has taken for someone to discover what such a needle can do. It has been in existence since the beginning of industrialisation, when thousands of such needles were used in the big needlefelting machines.

Most people know machine-made needlefelt in some form or other, and there is still plenty of it being produced. But today other materials than wool are also needled; glass fibre for boats, for example.

I have mainly described sculptural felting techniques incorporating soapy water in my two previous books. In this book I show how you can work completely without water, using only a felting needle to fix the wool to an existing spatial shape or base.

You can also choose to combine wetfelting and needlefelting by, for example, wetfelting the piece of background to a relief. But I have concentrated on showing the techniques I have developed for sculptural and pictorial felting.

First, the method of work for one model is described in detail, then followed by variations of this, shown in less detail.

You can read about my latest felting projects on my homepage, **www.feltmaking.dk**. A list of coming felting courses and lots of pictures are also to be found here, as well as the possibility of ordering felting needles and lots more.

Have fun,

Birgitte Krag Hansen

Materials

The material used for felting is washed and carded sheep's wool (batts). This can be bought in broad lengths ready for use – both for flat things, and for forming sculptural figures.

Carded wool is carded on machines that criss-cross the wool fibres in sheets that can be separated into suitably thin layers. The wool is available in many shades and mixtures of natural colour as well as in a large number of dyeings; see the list of suppliers at the back of the book.

Natural colours are good to use for the basic work as they give a good colour foundation. One can in this way give the surfaces a watercolour effect, with the base colour almost having the appearance of shading.

You can also card the wool yourself, and so have the chance of using some of the many exciting varieties of wool that exist. For example, hand cards can be used. These are particularly good for mixing colours, but would otherwise be too time-consuming to use. Another possibility is to use a hand-swung drum carder. You can also get a recommendable smaller engine-driven drum-carding machine for large amounts.

Suitable types of wool

In principle all types of wool can be used for needlefelting, but as with other kinds of felting one has to choose the wool in relation to the effect one wants to achieve. There are technical qualities in some types of wool, especially in relation to spatial shapes, that make them suitable for sculpting.

A type of wool that is particularly good for all kinds of needling is Finn wool that comes from a Finnish race of sheep. On the other hand, you ought to avoid merino wool in tops (narrow lengths originally intended for spinning). It is not good for shaping, and is not suitable for pictorial expression, either. Another disadvantage of merino wool is that the needle holes are too visible on the surface, and that the wool forms stripes. There is, of course, no rule without an exception – I use white merino to make eyes. There is also another kind of merino wool on the market, carded in broad lengths. This works well, and can be used especially for surfaces and for figures' clothing.

Wool for spatial shapes

It can be good to use a slightly coarse wool for the innermost core when one is needling spatial shapes, as it has a character that can contain air between the fibres. This means that the shape does not become too compact and hard while shaping it, but, instead, retains its mouldability throughout the process. Among others, Romney, Spelsau, Faeroe Island wool, and wool from many of the mixed races in Denmark, have these qualities.

Thin coverings of more fine-fibred wool are used for the coloured surfaces of the spatial shape.

Wool for flat felting

A relatively fine-fibred wool is good when felting reliefs and detailed landscapes – especially as a base and for thin lines. But coarse and raw wool are perfect for effect, also when used together with fine-fibred wool as a contrast. And if one has a fleece that has already felted itself at the base while still on the sheep, but retains a beautiful surface, this in itself makes a perfect base.

Other materials

It is also possible to needle many other materials in or on a needlefelted background. Various yarns can form patterns and frames, and a thread of metal and silk can, for example, be added to the material to give effect.

Equipment

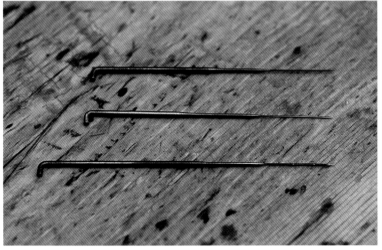 

Felting using a felting needle requires very little equipment:

Felting needles (see below). A needle holder with a number of needles is helpful, if one is felting bigger things.
A mat of foam rubber (not too soft), at least 5 cm thick. The size should correspond to the subject.
A big, sharp, darning needle.
Batts (carded wool).

Felting needles

There are many different kinds of felting needles, each of which has a special function. It can at first be difficult to tell one needle and its attributes from another. The needles seem much alike, but after having used them a while, one quickly senses that there is a big difference.

The sharp end is made of hard-fired steel, which means that it has been possible to make it extra sharp, and that it maintains this sharpness. The needle has three cuts down its sides like a leather needle. These cuts have oblique incisions (barbs) angled downwards towards the point of the needle.

When the needle is stuck into the woollen material the incisions get hold of the wool fibres and pass them down.

The more one needles, the more densely the fibres are »worked« together until they finally form a material that is so firm that it is impossible to rip it apart. This means that it is not necessary to finish it by felting with soapy water as one has normally done. If the material is needled enough, it will hold itself in place.

In most cases I needle with a single needle, but I use needle holders in order to needle with a number of needles simultaneously when working on big surfaces and figures.

There are also small needlefelt machines that can make felt lengths 50 to 90 cm wide. These machines are expensive to buy, and are used especially by professional felters.

I have used three needles in this book:

The ordinary needle (no. 1) (all-round needle) is a needle of medium thickness that can basically speaking be used for everything.

The silver needle (no. 2) is a little bit finer than the ordinary needle, and therefore makes smaller holes in the surface. It is suitable for flat felting – e.g. pictures, clothing, figures, and prefelting. It is an advantage to use a 5-needle holder for bigger things.

The star needle (no. 3) is the finest needle. It is good when applying very fine, thin lines, and is extremely good for doing eyes, and for working the surface. The star needle is constructed slightly differently than the other two needles because its incisions (barbs) are right at the point so that it does not pass the wool so deeply into the material. Furthermore, it has a star-shaped cross section in contrast to the other two needles that have a triangular one. The star shape results in the needle leaving smaller holes.

All three needles need to be used carefully as the hard-fired steel is brittle. If the needles are handled with care, so that one only pokes directly down into the material and does not pull them up sideways, they can last a number of years.

Felting needles can be bought from well-stocked hobby shops.

Needle holders
I also use two kinds of needle holders as well as the needles – a two-needle holder and a five-needle holder.

The two-needle holder is good when needling bigger, sculptural shapes, and it is also excellent for doing edges.

The holder with five needles is particularly suitable for pictures and background surfaces, and for the figures' clothing.

Functions of the felting needle

The basic function
The illustrations show how the needle passes more and more fibres down into the material, it thereby becoming denser and denser.

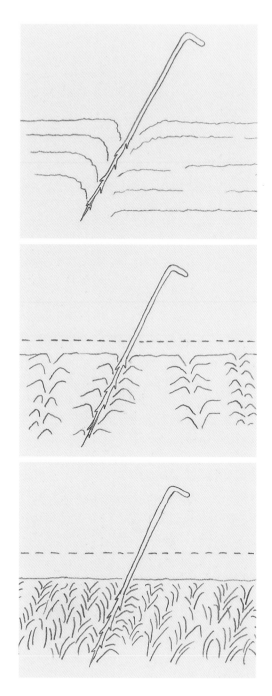

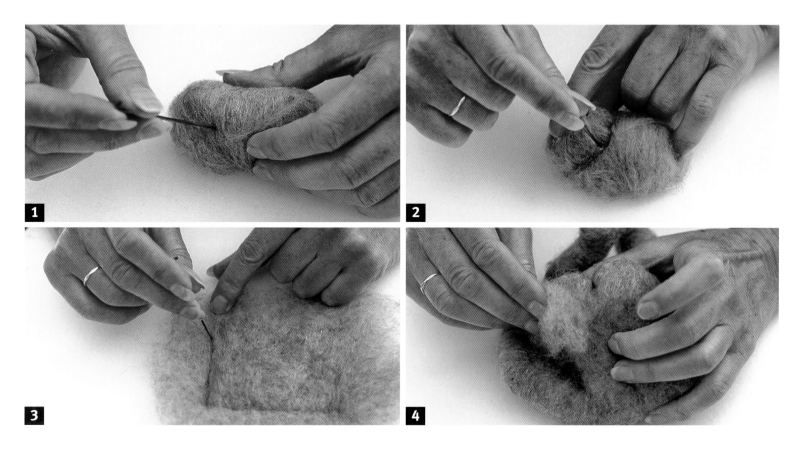

Different needling techniques

Surface needling

1. Here, the needle is only stuck into the very top layer, giving a dense, »closed« surface.

Deep needling

2. Here, the needle both shapes and makes the material firm and strong deep down. This method is also used to needle new shapes onto the basic shape, or to join two shapes.

Needling of lines for edges

3. Here, the needling is done so densely that is makes a line that can be used to edge a picture or clothing.

Addition of extra layers

4. Here, the shapes are given extra layers or covering layers that are needled on gradually.

In order to work freely, with no danger of the needle going into the table and breaking, use a mat of foam rubber at least 5 cm in thickness and not too soft as a base. Use this both when working with flat pieces and spatial shapes.

Test felting

Specific techniques and variations in shaping the wool will be used throughout this book. The descriptions in this section make it possible for you to become conversant with how to work with the wool.

There are basically three techniques:

- A technique used to roll shapes.
- A technique whereby a folding line is needled to a flat layer of carded fibres, which is then folded around the line.
- A technique whereby layers of wool are laid on top of each other like mattresses.

Rolling technique

An oval shape is rolled; preferably in the hand.

1. Hold a hand-sized piece of carded wool in the palm of your left hand. Grip the top edge and fold a couple of centimetres of it down over the wool, while pressing out the air.

2. Hold the folded edge firmly with your thumb, and fold the sides in at an angle so that a point is formed at the top.

3. Fold again from the top, taking a little at a time, remembering to press out all the air. Do this alternately until all the wool has been used.

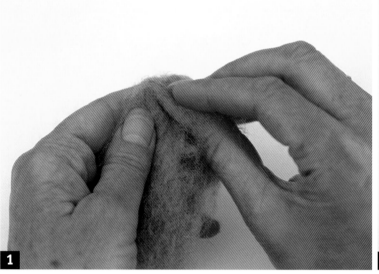

4. Needle the edge firmly by sticking the felting needle into the shape a number of times. Now take a new piece of carded wool. Place the ball shape on top of this piece, and continue rolling it to the size you need. After this give the surface a light needling. Now the shape is ready to be worked further e.g. to make a head.

5. Some of the rolled shapes (nose, breasts, bottom, rolls of fat etc.) are completed with the final end of wool hanging loose. This is to be used as an invisible link to the underlying surface that it gets attached to. This loose end should not be too thin, otherwise the link will be too abrupt.

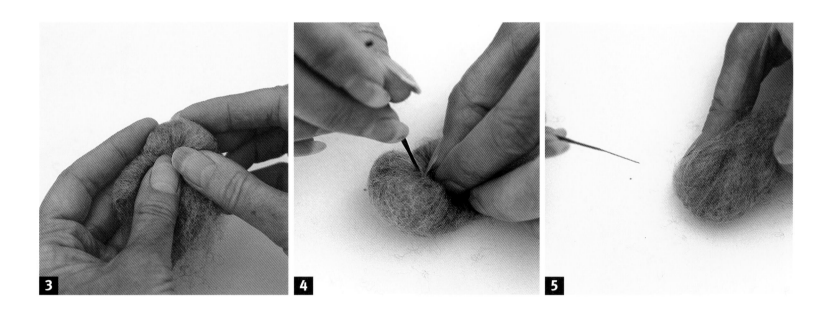

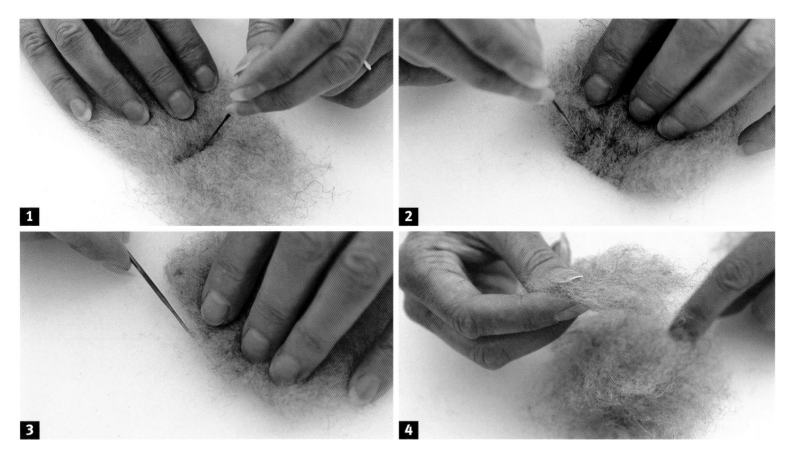

Flat felting technique

The flat felting technique is used first and foremost for making lips, but is also used to make eyelids, ears, edges etc.

1. Lay a suitably thin layer of carded wool onto the foam rubber mat, and needle a line along the middle of the wool so that you have a folding edge.

2. Fold the wool along the line, and needle densely along the edge.

3. Gently pull the wool off the foam rubber mat. The sheet has now got a hairy edge, which is removed by turning the reverse side up, using the felting needle to lay the fibres in over the edge while needling sideways.

The folded piece can now be needled together with another shape.

Mattress technique

The mattress technique is used for those places where one wishes to add more wool to the height, and where one wants to round off the edges.

4. Imagine you are building up a staple of carded fibre sheets – like mattresses on top of one another. This way you can make extremely small and big shapes (both in height and width) tailor-made for the place you need to use them.

Flat felting

Flat felting means that one works with a flat background of needled wool, onto which one needles a subject.

You can work totally flat, as in the case of the heart below, or you can make combinations in order to achieve greater or lesser relief effect.

Needlefelted heart

This flat heart shape is a good way to start. Here, you learn:

- To needle edges
- To make thin strings to form patterns
- To fill in shapes
- To use effects (gold thread, silk etc.)

Materials
– a 40 x 40 cm foam rubber mat, at least 5 cm thick
– an ordinary felting needle (no. 1) or a silver needle (no. 2), and a star needle (no. 3)
– carded wool in different colours
– silk and gold thread (optional)

1. Start by making some long, thin strings of wool for the patterns on the heart. These strings are made the same way as nomadic women do when making strings to form patterns on their carpets. Take a wad of carded wool in your left hand, and, using your right hand, pull a few fibres 2 to 3 cm in length out of the wad. Rub these fibres thoroughly between your fingers and repeat the process until the string is approximately 40 cm long. It is a good idea to begin with a dark colour.

2. Tear a heart shape out of a sheet of carded wool. Lay the heart on a foam rubber mat, and needle it a few times to this so that it lies flat. Avoid needling right out to the edge. Now densely needle a line all the way around, about 1 cm in from the edge. This line forms the final shape of the heart.

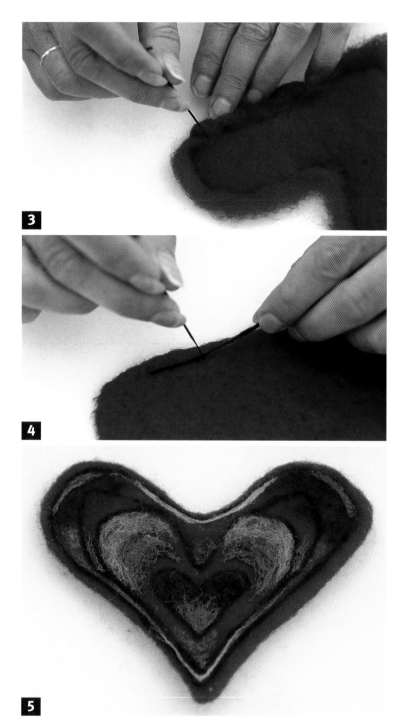

3. Fold the loose edge in tightly over the heart, and needle it firmly. Then needle the whole surface densely.

4. The pattern lines can now be added, using the star needle. Fix the end of the string by needling it, then hold it outstretched with your left hand while needling it onto the heart. The string is lengthened by needling on a new end. If desired, also needle on strings in other colours.

5. Spaces have now been made in the heart that can be filled in using a thin layer of other colours. Possibly put different colours into the same space – in small wads at a time – resulting in a rainbow effect.

Extra effects can be added, using shiny silk tops or nylon carded fibres. Perhaps add a few woollen fibres across these to help hold them in place. A metal thread can be felted in as a handle – also by using a finishing layer of wool.

When you have finished decorating the heart, needle everything very thoroughly to make it firm. The reverse side of the heart will appear woollen on removing it from the foam rubber mat. You can choose to keep the heart like this, or to fold the fibres down with the needle, needling them sideways into place, or you can iron it.

Woollen name plate

This small plate gives a very decorative effect, and can also stand hanging outdoors. It is an excellent, easy little idea as a present, where one can needle letters and patterns directly onto a needled background, using a variety of wool leftovers in every conceivable colour and quality.

Materials
– a 40 x 40 cm foam rubber mat, at least 5 cm thick
– an ordinary felting needle (no. 1) or a silver needle (no. 2)
– carded wool in different colours

1. First, needle a base consisting of a layer of carded wool of medium thickness, and needle in the edge like on the heart earlier. Needle on a frame by laying thick wool along the edge. A lot of needling is necessary to ensure that the frame is firm. It is also possible to needle a thinner thread along the thick one. The wool ends should overlap each other a little where they join.

2. Fill out the base by needling on thin layers of colour – e.g. try a division into quadrangles of different colours under each letter. You can also mix (blend) the colours using cards or your fingers. This gives an effective transition of colour.

3-4. Now shape the letters using threads of wool, and needle them in place. A woollen pattern can be added if there is extra space.

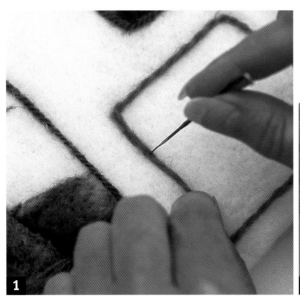

Flat felting with relief

Materials
- a 40 x 40 cm foam rubber mat, at least 5 cm thick
- an ordinary felting needle (no. 1) or a silver needle (no. 2)
- carded wool in different colours
- machine-made needlefelt (optional)
- a 5-needle holder (optional)

Flat needled landscape

A needlefelted background is a very rewarding material to work with when one is making small sketchlike pictures.

You can needle your background either out of natural-coloured carded wool or out of blended dyed wool. A good, subtle effect is achieved by needling on machine-made needlefelt that can be bought by the metre from 'Kartehuset' – see the list of suppliers at the back of this book.

The piece of needlefelted material is laid onto the foam rubber mat, and needled in place by needling densely. The edge is needled in the same way as the heart on pages 13 and 14.

You do not need to plan very much before you start. Felt has the quality of »suggesting« subjects immediately one begins adding a little colour to the background. Colour can be added either in one thin, unbroken layer or in small, tiny wads as though one is »painting« with wool.

1. Shape a frame either from a thin piece of rolled string or from a piece of wool of suitable colour and coarseness. You might needle a very thin layer into place as background colour. Preferably use a holder with a number of needles. This allows you to work faster, and makes the felt firmer. The subject could, for example, be a very simple tree with a trunk made up of brown wool that is first placed, and then needled on along the edges, giving the slight effect of relief.

2. Then add the branches by rolling thin lengths of string, as explained for the heart on page 13. Needle all of the pieces of string to the tree, and shape the branches as you needle them onto the background.

Picture 3 has two subjects on the same needled background. This example shows the same subject in two different seasons.

The subjects can also be of different size. Picture 4 shows three different subjects. A kind of cartoon effect is obtained regarding perspective by enlarging the subject in the background, making the result very striking. Perspective has also been used in picture 5.

Felt is also excellent to embroider on. Combining the two techniques gives a very beautiful effect.

This could be done by embroidering enlarged branches with leaves onto the background. Remember to use either machine-made needlefelt or very firmly needled felt if you intend embroidering on it.

Needled landscape with trees in relief

Here the flat, needled landscape has tree trunks and other details added to it, by fixing them in relief. It gives a very beautiful sense of depth, and shows how coarse and raw wool can give effects.

You can build up a landscape in an unlimited number of ways, and many rules can be made for this. But in this case the idea is that the landscape ought to develop spontaneously as you are working with it. The picture ought to come from within you and not be based on a photograph or a painting. You can extend the subject in all directions later if you keep getting ideas as things develop.

The idea of the picture is opened up by building up the background of the landscape in greater or smaller coloured sections that together (perhaps by chance) form an underlying atmosphere.

1. For example, let the top third section be of a white or very light grey batts, the middle section possibly of a medium brown, and the bottom section of a dark shade.

This division could be the beginning of almost anything – woodland, fields, coastline etc. – a kind of open start.

A good result is achieved if the three differently-coloured sections have uneven edges and vary in breadth. The picture edges can be folded in later.

The horizontal lines are the most important in this first phase of the picture, because they form the basic character of the landscape. The three coloured sections are needled together on the foam rubber board. It is advisable to use a needle holder as a lot of needling is required to assemble the surface.

2. The big sections can now have smaller ones added to them. These smaller, differently-coloured, horizontal pieces divide the landscape up even more. It might be advisable to start with some dark, thin, horizontal contour lines, and fill out the spaces formed.

You can easily try out the effect of the colours, removing some again, or adding more to moderate a colour.

You will almost certainly need many more shades while you are working. It is good to use cards for this, or your hands to blend the wool. You can mix an enormous number of shades from just a few primary colours by carding or blending them.

It can be difficult to judge when one has finished the sections, but it is always possible to continue with more colours, even after trees and the like have been added.

It is often difficult to add colours to the sky section without it seeming overdone. You can subdue the effect either by carding the light ground colour and the colour you have chosen together, or by adding a very thin layer of the ground colour on top of the applied colour.

If there is a horizon, a thin strip of white wool just above it adds great depth to the picture.

You can begin including vertical things to the picture when the added colours give a good basic atmosphere.

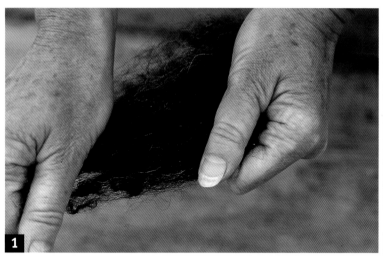

Different trunks

These trunks are meant to be added to a prepared, needled landscape background. This gives ample opportunity of using all the coarse types of wool – the coarser the better – resulting in some really fantastic trunks that have the proper physicality and effect.

1. The wool has to be carded before the trunks are shaped. This can be on a carding machine with a drum, or done using hand cards. However, it is also possible to do it just by teasing the wool, using one's hands to pull the fibres parallel.

Lay the wool on the foam rubber mat in the required shape and needle it together. Keep in mind that the trunk needs to be somewhat wider than one expects the result to be. The edges have to be folded in, and a little wool put underneath so that the trunk is given relief. If required, rip »tears« at the bottom of the trunk as roots. Extra perspective-effect is gained if the trunk is longer than the base. Possibly add a thin »veil« in another shade on part of the surface, so that the tree rounds slightly. Three different bark effects are now possible. These are made either by means of twisted shapes, coarse treads of wool, or staples.

Twisted shapes

2. Make the structure of bark by tightly twisting a wad of wool; possibly adding stripes of other colours to the wad. Needle the shape onto the trunk – starting at one end, then stretching it, and finally needling it into place at the other end.

You can make bark effects by placing the tightly twisted wads close together in vertical lines of varying height.

The wad of wool can also be needled on in a round or asymmetrical shape e.g. making it look like a scar.

3

4

5

Coarse threads of wool

3. Very beautiful structures can be obtained by needling treads of wool in vertical lines and allowing them to twine together. You should use a very coarse or unevenly spun thread for this.

The effect using threads of wool can also be combined with the tightly twisted wads of wool. These should be placed close together in vertical lines of varying height.

Raw wool

4-5. A special bark effect can be achieved using raw wool. The best result is obtained when you choose raw wool that is light at the tips. Start from the bottom, and needle it on staple by staple until the trunk is covered.

Stumps

6. To make a stump, needle a thick piece of wool that is so wide that it can be folded into a low, hollow cylinder. Try to place the fibres vertically, and perhaps add a moss colour or other colours to the surface for effect. You can also choose to rip up the bottom edge a bit to form »roots« at the base.

Possibly add a lighter layer inside to highlight the hollowness more strongly. Needle densely, fold the top edge down so that it becomes thick, and, finally, gather the side edges on the reverse side and needle them together. It is also possible to attach a light-beige coloured oval shape with annual rings, and needle this on along the top edge.

6

Needling trunks into place

Trees with thin lateral branches are needled directly onto the landscape, like this: Use a »sausage« of coarse wool that is so long and thick that the top part can be divided into branches. Needle the trunk onto the background by first needling along the sides. Divide the trunk up into branches that are needled into the landscape, then divide them again further out and needle into place. When all of the wool has been securely needled, extra thin lateral branches can be added if deemed necessary.

Some trees are first completely needled on the foam rubber mat, and afterwards placed in the landscape, so that the edges are folded inwards and the trunk lies so that it bulges from the surface. If necessary, put a little bit of wool in under the trunk to keep the relief form. After this, needle the tree on along its edges, and perhaps add a few vertical lines on the trunk.

These trunks can themselves be the major subjects in a picture with quite a neutral background. Some amusing effects can also be obtained from incorporating trolls or animal faces into a trunk.

Sketch models

It is often an advantage to needle small sketch models before starting on a big subject such as an illustrated story. These models can later become bigger and more worked out versions.

Needled faces can be made very different e.g. by varying the size of noses and eyes, and the placing of facial features. Highly-raised eyebrows and a slightly open mouth give an expression of awareness, for example.

Skin colour can have unlimited variety, and assist in giving figures very distinctive characteristics.

Human faces

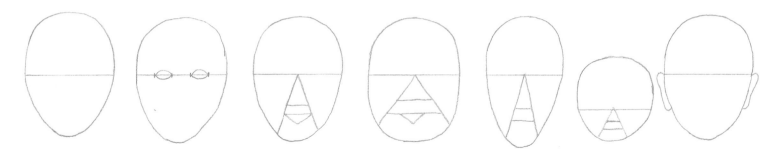

You do not have to follow a whole lot of rules concerning distance and placing of facial features in relation to each other when building up a face. One is too easily tied down by such rules, thereby forfeiting the freedom of working with one's own self-expression. There are a few simple, useful guidelines, however:

The line on which the eyes are placed divides the head-shape into two equal parts.

Five eyes make up the width of head, so determining the size of the eyes ought not to be difficult.

You can alter size, height, and width by dividing the face up into triangles, and thus find the desired shape.

Examples of triangle variations are shown above: an ordinary face, a broad face, a Red Indian one, and a child face.

The tips of the ears should be at approximately the same height as the narrowest part of the bridge of the nose. The lowest part of the ears should be in line with the upper lip.

The illustrations below show the characteristics of different kinds of expression – angry, smiling, laughing, worried, supercilious, and lethargic.

Building a face

Felting a face is one of the most exciting aspects of needlefelting. This section shows how a face is built up step by step.

You can choose to make a face with very simple features – and with eyes having only a few details – and yet achieve a very elegant result. Or you can make use of all the many detailed possibilities shown here.

The face is here shown on a round shape. A face for a relief is built up in the same way, though started slightly differently, see page 62.

The rule when building a face is that the whole part from the eyes down should be made as a »loose« mask that can be lifted out of the basic shape. This allows a much greater number of possibilities for making different expressions, because the part of the mouth is shaped independently.

Materials
– a 40 x 40 cm foam rubber mat, at least 5 cm thick
– an ordinary felting needle (no. 1) or a silver needle (no. 2)
– a big, sharp darning needle
– a thin straw
– carded wool in a natural colour for the basic shape, a chosen skin colour, and various colours for lips, eyes, and effects.

Head-shape

1. Roll an egg-shaped ball of carded wool in a neutral colour as described in the section rolling technique on pages 10-11. The easiest size to work with is a head of about 9 cm. Needle an even surface and mark the middle line.

Nose

2. Roll a tight ball as described in the section rolling technique on pages 10-11, and leave the end hanging loose. Keep the shape together by needling the back.

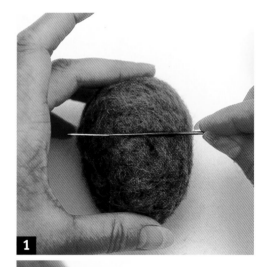

3. After this, roll a cylindrical shape for the bridge of the nose, and needle it lightly.

4. Place the cylinder on the reverse side – close against the ball.

5. Fold the edges in over the cylinder and needle them on – let the end with the bridge of the nose remain loose, and spread it out in a fan shape.

6. Put the nose on the head-shape so that the part that is fan-shaped reaches above the middle line.

7. Needle the nose into place, stitching deeply at the two points for the corners of the eyes.

8. Give the uppermost, loose fan-shape some light, surface needling so that it is flattened onto the head-shape.

The nose is shaped further after the lips and cheeks have been put on.

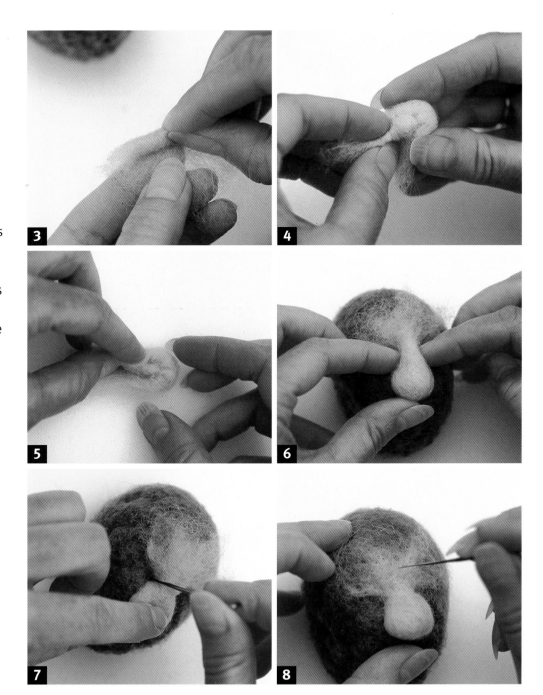

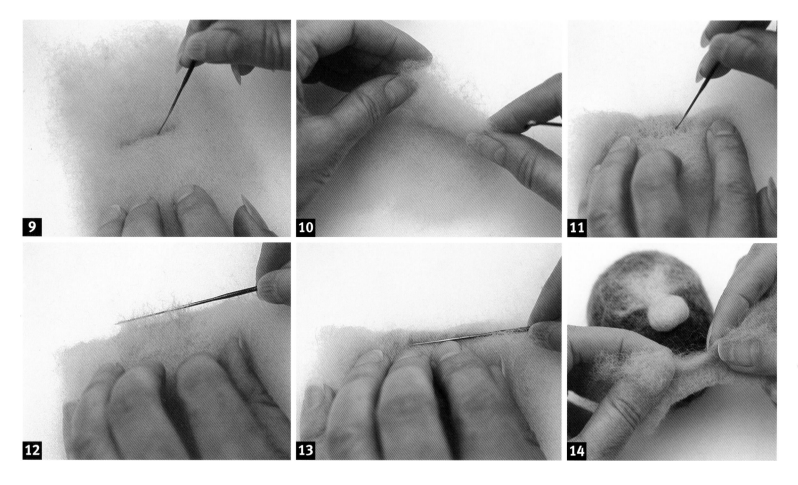

Lips

The lips are made using the flat felting technique, see page 12. Think of the upper lip as a flap of skin attached to the underside of the nose.

9. Lay a piece of carded wool of suitable thickness, with a width equivalent to that of the face, onto the foam rubber mat. Needle a dense line, a little wider than the nose, in the middle of the wool.

10. Let the wool remain fixed to the rubber foam mat, and fold the piece together over this needled line.

11. Needle a flat piece from the edge along the needled line and down. Needle densely at a height equivalent to the upper lip. Be careful not to needle too broadly, otherwise the result is an ape-like appearance.

12. Pull the upper lip gently from the foam rubber mat. This leaves a hairy edge where the line was needled. Turn the reverse side up, and lay the lip down on the foam rubber mat. Pass the felting needle in under the hairs and bend them in over the edge.

13. Needle the hairs sideways into the flat piece.

14. Make the upper lip ready for attachment by ripping a tear in the middle, right down to the needled piece.

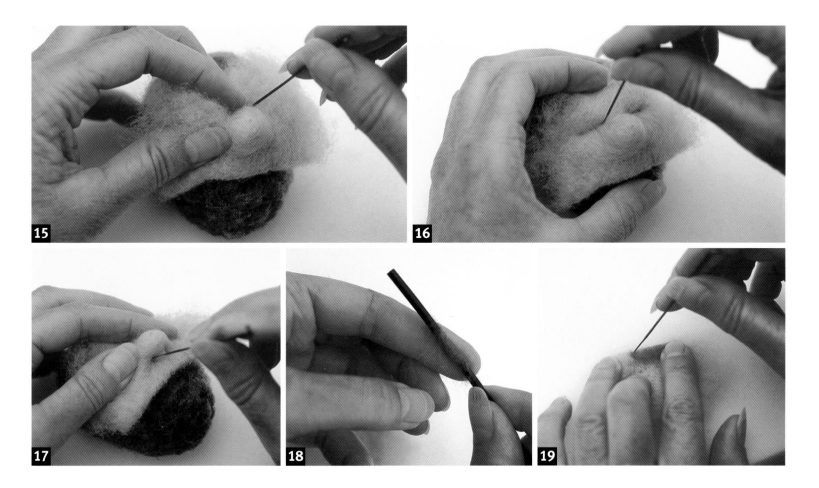

15. Now attach the lip firmly under the nose and along the sides. Be careful about turning the fibres that have to be attached under the nose *outwards*. The edges are placed up along the nose, and are fixed to the same two points as the nose was.

16. Then needle outwards from this point in a horizontal line corresponding to the lowest part of the eye.

17. Needle the piece firmly onto the underside of the nose by stitching up into the two points where the nostrils are to be formed.

The lower lip is felted the same way as the upper lip, but in this case colour is added to the lower lip during felting. After folding, a line is needled, forming a lip shape. Then, needle densely just under this shape.

18. Take a very small wad of lip colour, roll it tightly around your straw, and pull it off.

19. Place the rolled lip colour onto the lip shape, and needle it on.

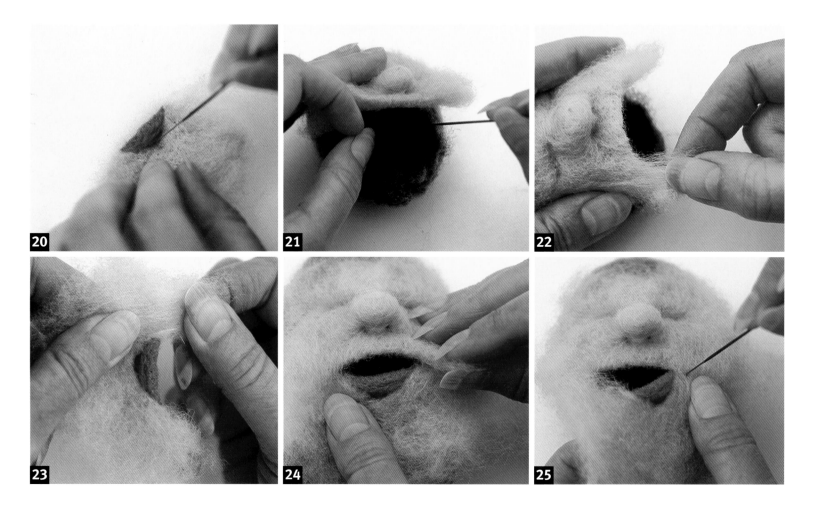

20. If required, take a very small wad, a little darker than lip colour, roll it between your fingers, and needle it on exactly under the middle of the lip. A little can also be needled to the sides to make shadow, giving an exciting effect. Pull the lip from the foam rubber mat, turn the reverse side up, and needle the hairy edge well out of the way as with the upper lip. Bend the lip in the middle so that a v-shape is formed giving a happy expression.

21. Needle a completely thin sheet of dark-brown wool into place inside on the egg-shape under the upper lip. This gives perspective when one looks into the mouth.

22. Pull the fibres at the side of the upper lip down so that the folded edge is smoothed out to get it ready to be joined together with the lower lip.

23. Pull up the fibres at the sides of the lower lip so that the folded edge is smoothed out.

24. Place the upper lip on top of the lower lip.

25. Hold the two pieces up and needle them together so that they do not get attached to the basic shape.

26. Needling has to be done both from above and below.

27. When you place the upper and lower lips together, you can form the mouth as big and open as you want, giving it the shape that suits the expression you require. The mouth can be shaped crooked and sneering, round and shouting, singing etc. Try out the alternatives. The final shaping of the mouth can be done by needling it higher or wider.

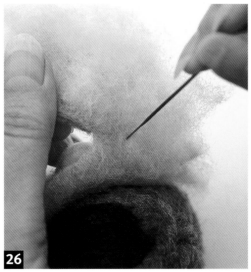

26

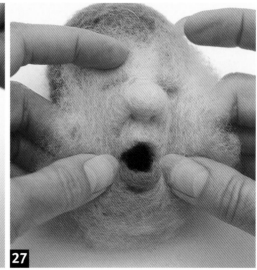

27

Chin

If you want extend the lower part of the face to make a witch-like appearance with the chin sticking out, or if you want the upper lip to protrude, do the following: Roll a shape, or several on top of each other, and needle them onto the basic shape so that they hold

the loose lower part of the face in the position you want it.

This is the moment when the loose lower part of the face has to be secured to the basic shape. If you have not formed a chin in the way just described, then do the following:

28. Roll a small shape for an ordinary chin.

29. Needle the shape onto the head-shape, and lay the loose lower part down and around this chin shape.

30. Needle the piece into place, the width of the chin.

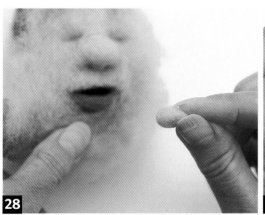

28

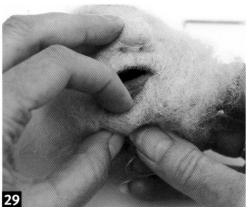

29

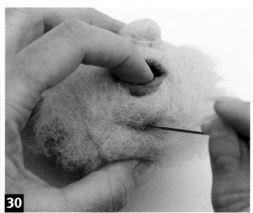

30

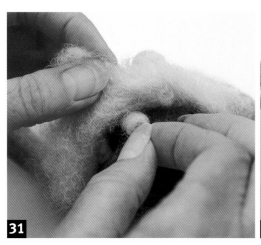

31

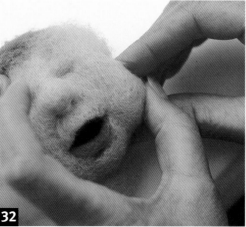

32

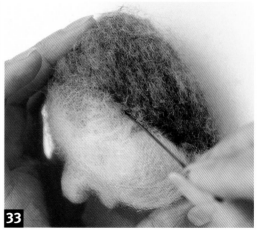

33

Cheeks

There are many different shapes to cheeks. A smile can be made, by forming tiny round shapes and needling them onto the egg-shape just outside the corners of the mouth.

You can also roll shapes as high cheekbones, placed under the eyes at the highest point of the cheeks, or you can shape big, round pouches that give a childlike or an apple-cheeked, jovial appearance.

31. Place the chin shapes under the loose lower part of the face from the side, and needle them on.

32. Pull the loose layer over the attached shapes and secure them on the side along the jaw line.

33. You can add a piece, if this layer is not wide enough.

Mouth

34. Begin by adding colour to the upper lip: Roll a little lip colour round your straw, pull it off, put it on the bottom edge of the upper lip and needle it into place so that it is completely narrow at the corners of the mouth.

35. Shape the mouth, and possibly needle quite a thin line along the edge of the lip.

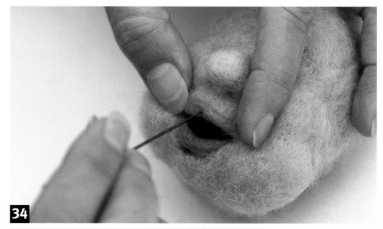

34

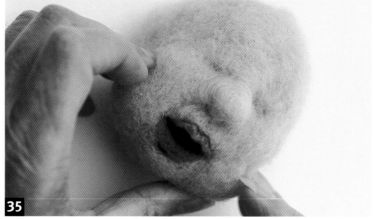

35

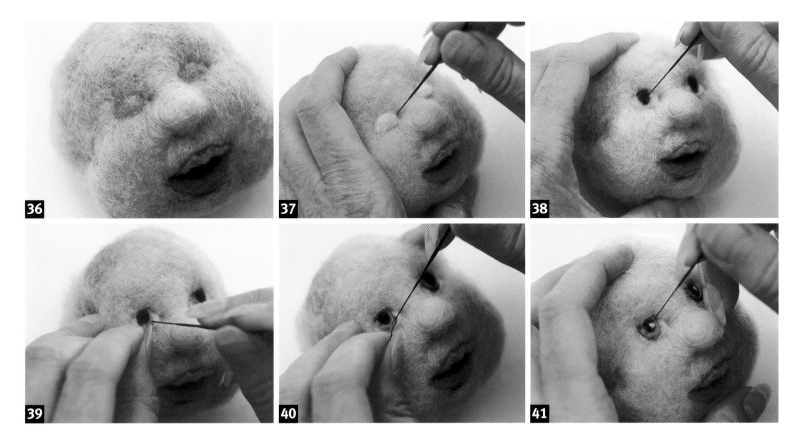

Eyes

The eyes are very important, and can be vital to the final result. You must aim to keep the eye as simple as possible, while at the same time making use of a few effective details. It is an advantage to use the star needle for this as it can work with very thin lines.

As described on page 25, you can work out the size of the eyes by imagining there has to be room for five eyes across the face.

36. Begin by marking out the eyes, needling their outline.
37. Make an eye shape using a thin sheet of white wool (preferably merino that is dense and very white), and then needling this sheet into place along its edge.

38. After this, shape a thin oval sheet of dark brown wool, and needle this to the white base. No white ought to be visible above the brown shape, otherwise the eye will seem to be staring. If you want a simple eye, skip the next two stages and continue from there.
39. Roll quite a thin but not too dark strip of colour to use as the iris. Needle this strip into place along the dark oval shape, excepting the top.
40. Now find an even darker colour that matches the colour of the iris, and pull a few fibres out of it. Roll this into an even thinner strip than the iris, and needle this into place as a contour line along the edge of the iris.
41. Roll a very tiny white ball as highlight in the eye, place it on the dark-brown piece a little off middle, put the star needle in its edge and needle it into place.

42. Roll a thin dark-brown strip to use as the line forming the lowest edge of the upper eyelid. First needle this into place at the corner of the eye, and hold it so that it remains outstretched while needling further. Continue needling the strip into place above the eye so that it just cuts off the uppermost part of the round iris, as an eyelid does. Try varying the way the line is put on. If it is angled, the eye is given a sleepy look etc.

You can give the eyes many expressions by placing the parts mentioned here differently: glance to one side, look up etc.

Eyelids, corners of the mouth, pouches, wrinkles and noses

Eyelids
Eyelids can be made in two ways.

43. The simplest way is to needle on a little colour just over the dark, thin line that marks the lowest edge of the eyelid.

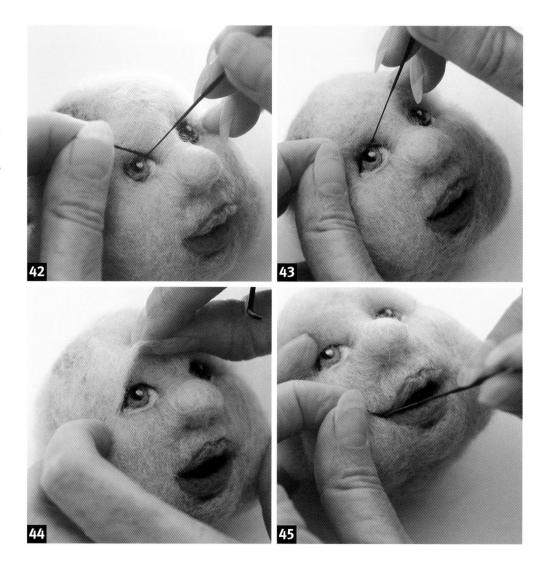

44. Loose eyelids can give a big effect for some figures – e.g. witches, trolls, and old people. Needle a tiny flat piece of very, very thin, carded wool as shown under flat felting technique on page 12. Let the folded edge form the shape of the eyelid, lay it on, and needle it into place from the nose up above the eye.

Corners of the mouth
45. Roll a very, very thin dark brown piece of string (see page 13) and lay one end of it in the mouth, needling it into place. The other end should go out as a thin line that completes the corner of the mouth a little outside of the lip colour.

Pouches under the eyes and wrinkles
46. Roll a piece of thin, carded wool around a straw, so that the roll is turned outwards.

47. Needle the shape into place under the eye.

48. This technique can also be used to form wrinkles on the face, including smile wrinkles.

Wing of the nose
49. Needle a shape like that of an eyelid, and needle it into place on the side of the nose, while folding the side of the shape in.

Bridge of the nose
50. Roll a cylindrical shape and needle it in the middle. Spread the ends out, lay the shape on the nose, needle it into place, and give it a thin finishing layer.

Long aquiline nose
A long aquiline nose can be made, by rolling a cylinder that is a little longer than the nose. Lay it on the nose so that one end bends down around the tip of the nose, needle it into place, and give it a thin finishing layer.

Witch/troll nose
For this, make a nose like the one explained on page 27, and then form an extra nose in the same way as the first one. The new nose is put on top and needled into place. Finally, the nose is given a thin finishing layer that is needled into shape.

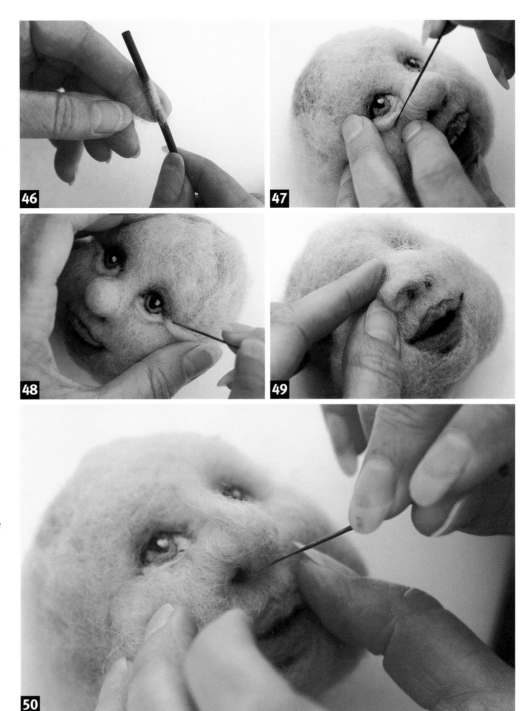

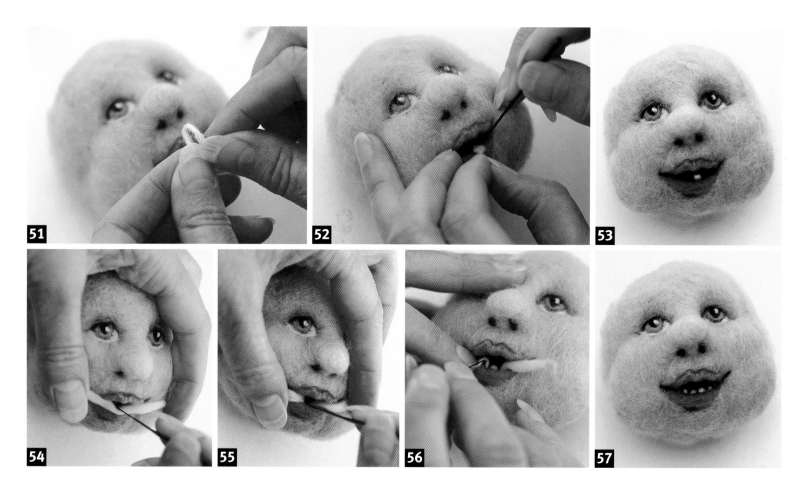

Teeth

Teeth are one of the hardest things to get to look right. There are three methods.

The easy ones

51. Roll a little piece of white »string«, and fold it double.

52. Needle the root into place.

53. The figure has now got a single tooth. With patience, you can make all of the teeth this way.

Instead of a piece of »string« you can roll a ball, and needle it into place.

The more difficult ones

54. Take a strip of white wool (preferably merino) that is wider than the mouth, and roll it. Lay it across the mouth.

55. Needle it into place in the middle just inside the lip, while holding the ends outstretched.

56. Form a little arch, and needle it into place. Continue this with the next teeth.

57. The figure has now got a whole row of teeth in the lower part of its mouth.

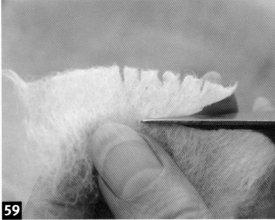

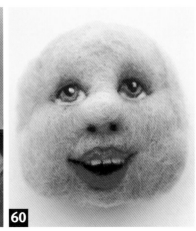

58 **59** **60**

The detailed ones
This final method is the most tricky, but is also the best.

58. Lay down the wool (preferably merino) as a thin strip.
Fold the strip together in the middle, pour on soapy water, lay
a piece of net over, and felt. Cut *very* small incisions in the
edge, and felt again.
59. Cut off some of the loose edge, let the wool dry, and
needle the piece into place in the mouth.
60. The figure has now got a whole row of teeth in the upper
part of its mouth.

The »safest« thing is to put teeth in the lower part of the mouth. It is more
difficult to make them look natural in the upper part of the mouth.

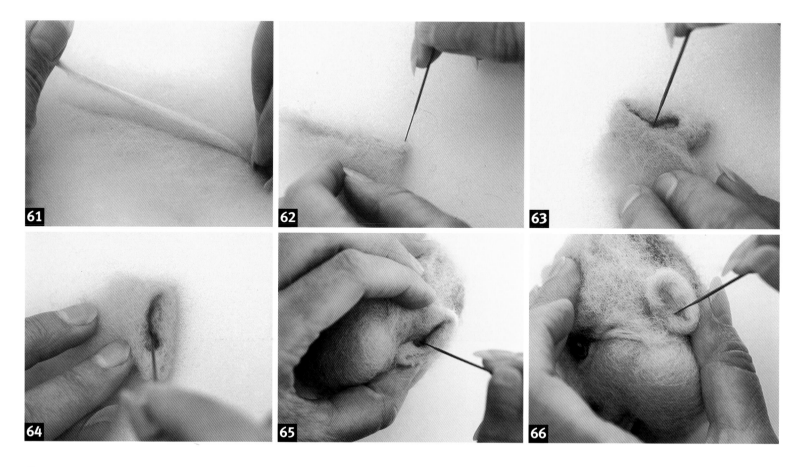

Ears

Try judging whether the forehead part is high enough before putting on the ears. If not, you can needle sheets of wool on, while pressing out the air. Maybe more wool also needs to be needled on for the neck.

61. Needle down through the middle of a narrow strip of wool. Roll a thin, compact sausage, and needle this into place on the line. Fold the wool in over it and needle everything together, so that the sausage forms the edge. The top part of the loose edge should not be needled.

62. Fold the lowest part up, and needle it into place alongside the edge.

63. Fold the upper edge down, and needle it into place a little in so that the fold is open.

64. Possibly put a little shading in the ear.

65. Open the loose edge, and needle the ear into place while forming it. Make the other ear the same way.

You can also make a simpler ear:

66. Roll a compact sausage of wool, and shape it into a semicircle. Needle this together, and needle it on just behind the cheekbone. Make the other ear the same way.

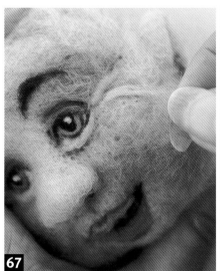
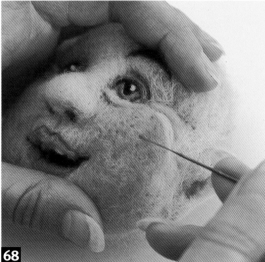
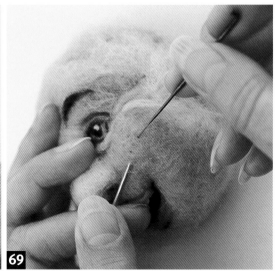

Colouring and finishing of the surface

Materials
– a star needle
– a big, sharp darning needle
– carded wool in different colours

Surprisingly little is needed when adding colour – especially when it is the skin. And if you add it in tiny wads, you can mix the colours and make shadows at the same time. You can also vary this by teasing the colours together by hand, or by carding them together.

Laying on colour using this technique gives something of the same effect as when one paints with oils or watercolours, because one can lay lots of thin layers on top of one another and, nevertheless, see through them.

If a colour appears too bright, it can be subdued by adding a little of the skin-coloured wool (possibly mixed with the original base colour) on top. Also try more vivid colours.

Choose a well-defined area – in this case the cheek:

67. Imagine where the light is coming from, and add the lightest colours where the light makes contact.
68. Needle the colours on in tiny wads like small brush strokes. It may even be necessary to break the wool fibres in order to make the portion small enough.

Initially, needle the colours on lightly – do not go in too deeply, otherwise the colour is concentrated in dots. When all the colours have been added, the surface has to be given a lasting finish:

69. Use the needle sideways (horizontally) in order to needle a firm skin surface. Having a darning needle in your left hand can be a great help in maintaining the shape. Push it just under the surface of the skin layer, and use it to hold the layer up while you are needling. Continue until you have a good, definite feeling that the fibres will not fluff when you brush them up. Complete one little area at a time before continuing.

Hair

Materials
– tops
– raw wool, perhaps coloured

Hair is an important completion of a figure, and can prove vital. Firstly, it can »save« a figure. Secondly, it can contribute by emphasising a good figure even more.

In many cases you will find that natural-coloured raw wool is what most obviously suits the figure. You can be so fortunate as to find pieces of wool hanging together that are only felted at the base but have fine staples on the surface. These pieces are ready for needling on as a wig by stitching between the staples. You can also needle on the hair staple by staple by putting the root end onto the base of the head and needling it a number of times, while holding it with your other hand.

70. Rainbow-coloured raw wool is also excellent as hair. It can be needled in the same way as raw wool (see above) if it is in one whole piece. Also see above how staples are to be needled on.

71. An attractive effect can be obtained from using tops, which look a lot like human hair. Rip off a suitable piece, place it on the head, and arrange it. Lift up the front edge, and needle along what is the equivalent of the hairline. Likewise, lift up what is at the neck, and needle along the hairline here. Lay the edge down again, and now needle the surface in broken, vertical lines. Finally, massage the surface so that the hair gains a natural appearance.

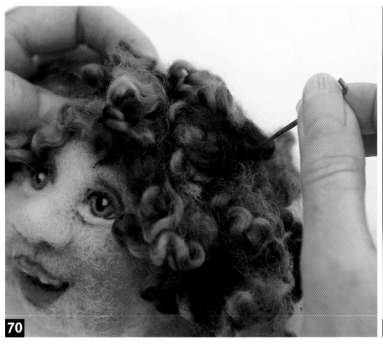

70

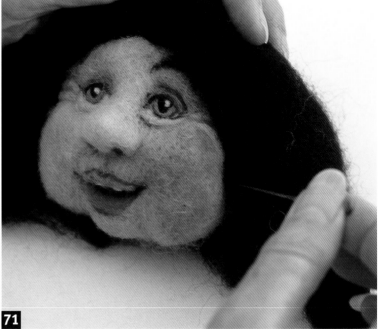

71

Here you can see how the very coarse wool used as hair helps give both the troll and the witch the right appearance. Pieces of tangled wool that already form wigs have been used.

Also notice the coarse wool that has been used to needle the faces. This emphasises the primitive look.

The little intuitive figure

This model is a funny, surprising figure that is easy to make, while also giving one the »bonus« of some amusing shapes.

Materials
- a 40 x 40 cm foam rubber mat, at least 5 cm thick
- an ordinary felting needle (no. 1)
- a thin straw
- carded wool in a neutral colour for the basic shape, a little coloured wool for the surface

Roll and needle five completely different shapes of carded wool. Try not to think of shapes like head, body and arms. Just roll and needle!

1. Needle these shapes together in totally random order as though they had been thrown on.

Nose

2. Choose one of the shapes as the head. Roll a nose (see page 27), and needle it onto the chosen head-shape.

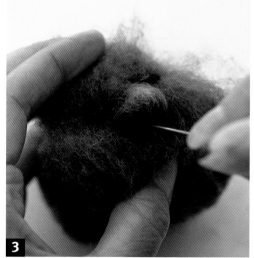

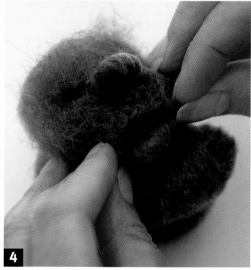

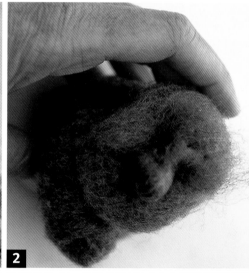

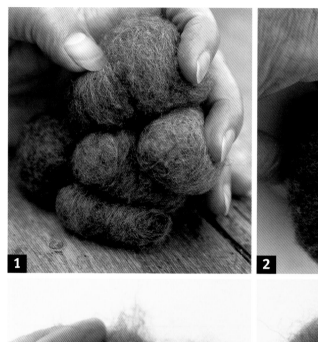

Upper lip

3. Needle an upper lip, see page 28. Divide it in the middle, and fix it around the nose.

Lower lip

4. Roll a little wad of wool round the straw. Work it off, and needle it into place under the upper lip.

5

Eyes

5. Get a little wad of dark wool, and needle it into the shape of an eye. Needle a little strip of white wool along one of the sides.

Ears

For this, roll a sausage that is thicker than the lower lip, and three times its length. Shape it into a semicircle as you are needling it on.

Hair

Make the hair by needling one or more wads of wool onto the top of the head.

Perhaps the little fellow is already finished, but if not, you can continue needling, and perhaps »discover« a hand or foot and finish off shaping it

with the needle. You could possibly needle a little colour onto the surface, and finish off by needling densely so that this surface becomes strong.

These two small funny intuitive beings have got their special personalities from the chance way the different parts of their bodies have been joined. The more impulsive the better.

Needlefelted figures

The making of needlefelted figures has a very flexible technique that is remarkably easy to work with. It is a development of the small beings I have made earlier, but it has gained many more possibilities now that one can use the felting needle for this technique. The results are always good.

Three figures, each with different degrees of difficulty, are shown here.

The easy one

This little figure is quite simple, and easy to use as practice. It is suitable for small trolls, pixies, and other beings.

Materials
- a 40 x 40 cm foam rubber mat, at least 5 cm thick
- an ordinary felting needle (no. 1)
- a thin straw
- carded wool in a neutral colour for the basic shape, a little coloured wool for the surface
- wool for the hair

1. Roll a head, a body, two arms, two legs, and two feet from lengths of carded wool. These lengths ought not to be too thin or too long – it is better they are added to in the process. The air should be pressed out of the wool as it is being rolled. Each of the shapes has to be needled densely and deeply to make it solid. This is not so for the arms. On the contrary, they need to be soft and bendable.

1

2. Needle the shapes together so that the figure is either sitting or standing. The legs are needled into place well up on the body by first needling along the edges. After this the needle is stuck through the middle of the leg and into the shape for the body. The head and the arms are needled on in a similar way.

3. When the parts are joined, extra wool can be added on for stomach and bottom, see the roll technique on pages 10 and 11.

4. Choose a colour as a finish. Carding the colours together or just teasing them together by hand so that they are mixed gives a good effect for trolls. The figure can be laid on a layer and the wool pulled tightly together around it, or this finishing layer can be needled into place by surface-needling small parts of it at a time. It is possible to fold the arms in over the body and needle them into place after they have been finished. You can needle the shape a lot more after the figure has been joined. For example, the knees and elbows can be needled in.

5. Form the hands from the lowest part of the arms, make the thumbs using the straw, and indicate the other fingers using the needle.

6. Needle the feet on, and also make the toes using the straw, or make small balls.

The face is built up in the way that is explained on pages 24 to 40, or as explained for the intuitive figure on pages 42 and 43.

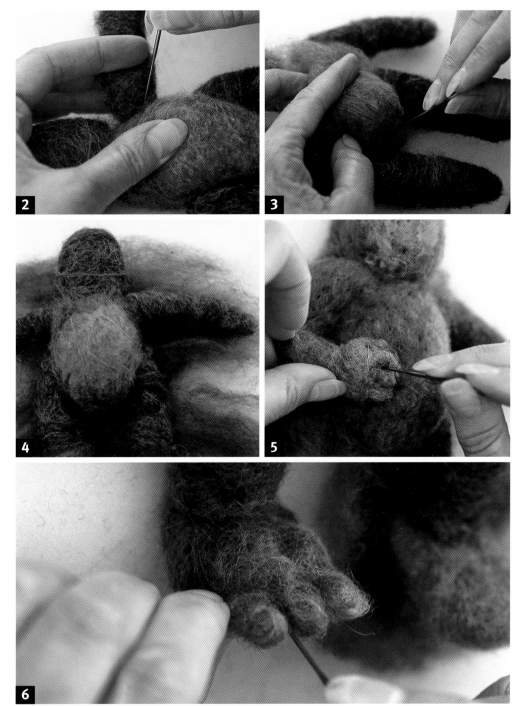

45

Here we see a couple of small, simple pixies, where the arms and legs are bent into shape last of all. Doing this ensures that the pixies crawl in the way crawling pixies should. The heads are put on so that the two pixies »talk to each other«.

Small, easy trolls are always a success, both with and without colour added. Trolls do not demand many details before looking alive. The hair can be anything from a big wig to just a little tuft on top of the head.

The good one – with many variations

This technique really gives a lot of possibilities, which you can play with and try out before deciding what the final position is to be. Moving the various parts of the body about can often give quite surprising results. The exciting thing of it is that there is no difficulty at all in finding natural positions that you would certainly never find through drawing.

It is best if the finished figure is at least 26 cm in height.

Materials
– a 40 x 40 cm foam rubber mat, at least 5 cm thick
– an ordinary felting needle (no. 1), or a silver needle (no. 2)
– a big, sharp darning needle
– a thin straw
– carded wool in a neutral colour for the basic shape (one of medium quality is good, but keep in mind that you can also use the completely coarse kinds of wool, which are extra good for sculpting)
– a chosen skin colour, a few colours for the surface

1. Roll and needle all the parts firmly (as explained in the section on the easy method on pages 44 and 45). At some stage lay all of the parts as seen in the picture, to see whether or not they are suitable. The topmost part of the body is a piece for the shoulder that makes the shoulder square. The piece is rolled into a flat, oval sheet form that is needled and attached to the body shape. Keep in mind that the parts for both arms and legs need to narrow towards the bottom end.

1

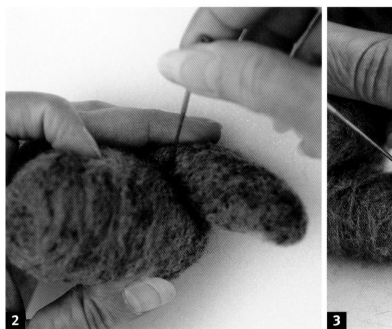

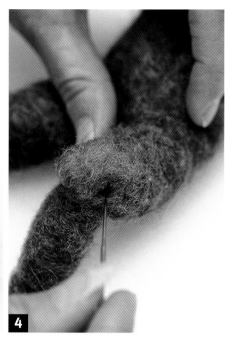

Legs

The thighs are put on right up on the body shape, so that the top of each almost reaches the waist. The thighs therefore ought to have a little extra length.

Hold the thighs tightly against the body and try out different positions. When the chosen position has been found, needle the part of each thigh that should touch the body so that it becomes a little flat.

2. Press the flat piece in against the body, and needle along the edge until the leg is fixed. Needle a little diagonally so that the indentations do not become too visible. Bending the inside of the thigh outwards from the body a little is necessary to be able to needle along the edge. The centre of the thigh is also needled by pushing the needle right through the thigh into the body. It is important to needle a lot of times, but without pulling the needle completely out each time as this makes the thigh flat.

3. After this, needle that part of the thigh flat where the lower leg is to sit. That is, if the lower leg bends to the side, then the thigh has to be needled on its side. If the figure is standing, place the lower leg behind the thigh. An easy way of fixing on the lower leg is by laying the thigh down onto the foam rubber mat and then needling along the edge. The outer point of the thigh should jut out over the lower leg a little so that it can be folded in to make the kneecap.

4. Form the kneecap by folding it down over the lower leg and needling it into place in a v-shape.

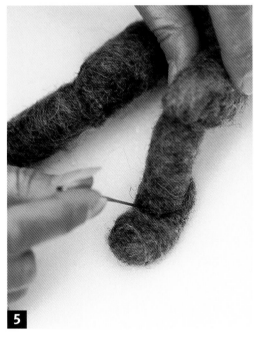

Feet

Roll a compact, flat oval shape that is thick, and widest at the toe for the feet.

5. Needle this onto the lower leg, first from above …
6. … and then under the foot.

Provide the foot with an instep by adding extra filling, as explained in section mattress technique on page 12. The amount ought to be very little in width so the wool fibres must be broken, if necessary.

Roll a shape for the heel as explained in section rolling technique on pages 10 and 11. Place the rolled end in as a heel cushion, lay the loose end up over the Achilles, and narrow it by needling.

Finally, needle the foot into shape, giving it an arch.

The toes are made in the same way as the fingers (see the next page), just shorter.

Arms and hands

When the required position has been found, needle the arms on as done with the legs. Remember to put the arms on high up so that the square-shape of the shoulder is retained.

The elbows are made in the same way as the knees.

The palms of the hands are made, by twining an oval shape at the end of each lower arm, and needling it on. Instead, you can use the bottom part of the lower arm as a palm if it is long enough. Needle a lot of times so that a thin wrist is formed.

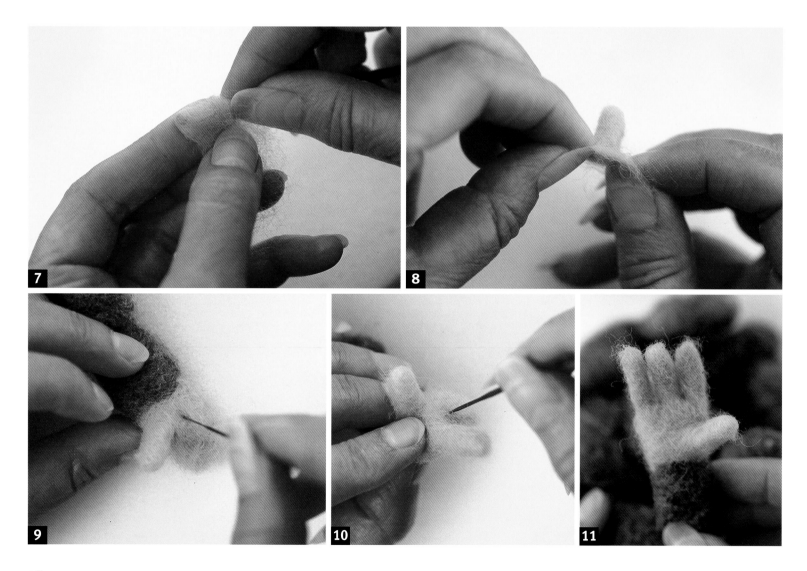

Fingers

Up until now neutral-coloured carded wool has been used for needling. Now you can change to skin-coloured wool.

7. Place the straw on top of a little piece of carded wool so that a side of the piece of carded wool hangs out of one end of the straw as shown. Fold the edge of the wool in over the straw, and roll, holding the wool closely against the straw. The end has also to be folded in every time so that it comes to form a fingertip. Pull out the straw, and needle the surface of the closed end as long as you want the finger to be.

8. Spread out the loose end.

9. Needle the finger to the palm of the hand. The thumb has to sit on the underside of the hand.

10. Felt the other fingers in the same way.

11. Four fingers are enough. You can place the fingers at the angle you want from the start.

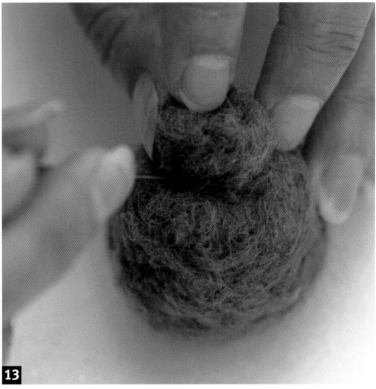

Finishing layer

When the figure is joined together, all the joints are covered with a thin layer of carded wool:

12. Take a thin, narrow strip and wrap it once round the joint – the wool must nestle against the shape without tightening it. Needle the finishing layer into place, needling it at an angle so that the joint is not visible.

Head

Do not put on the head until the face is made.

Try out the possible variations of head position. In most cases it will be sufficient to needle the head directly onto the body. But if you want the figure to have a neck, do the following:

13. Roll and needle a little cylindrical shape, and needle it firmly to the head along its edge. After this needle it down onto the body, also by needling along its edge. Finally, needle a number of times down through the centre of the neck shape, and give it a finishing layer.

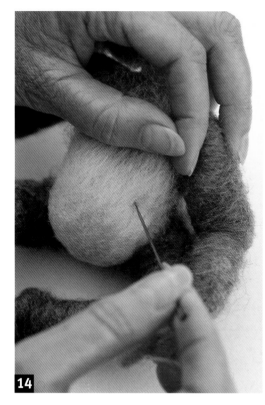 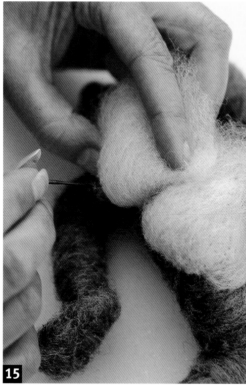 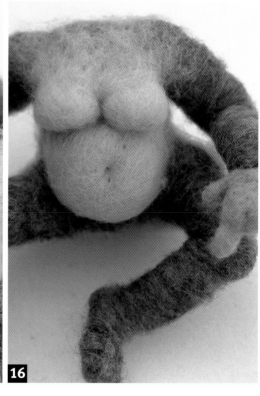

Outer shapes

When the whole figure has got its basic shape, you can begin giving it its outer shapes.

14. For the *stomach* roll a shape with a loose end for the finishing off, see the rolling technique on pages 10 and 11. Needle the shape on with the loose end up.

15. For the *bottom* roll two shapes using the same technique, but fold the lowest part of the side that is to face in towards the middle an extra time before attaching it. Fold the other side the opposite way and press it tightly against the first shape. Let the loose edge overlap the first shape so that the joint is hidden.

16. Roll the *breasts* in the same way and place them closely together (as the bottom) so that the chest remains flat. Needle in a little extra at the top beside the breast, and notice the line (the shape) out towards the arm.

17. To make the *shoulder blades* and the *chest,* fold sheets of carded wool, allowing the folded edges to meet in the middle. After needling the sheets into place, a thin finishing layer can perhaps be laid over the middle.

You can now choose to continue working with the shape if you wish.

18. If you want a full-bodied lady/gentleman lay on extra wool, e.g. for the hips ...

19. ... and rolls of fat, see the rolling technique on pages 10 and 11. You can use the mattress technique (see page 12) that levels out in all directions for thighs and lower legs. All you have to do, if the first shape is not big enough, is to put another lay on top.

20. If you do not want the figure to wear clothes, needle the surface so it is finished, see treatment of the surface on page 39.

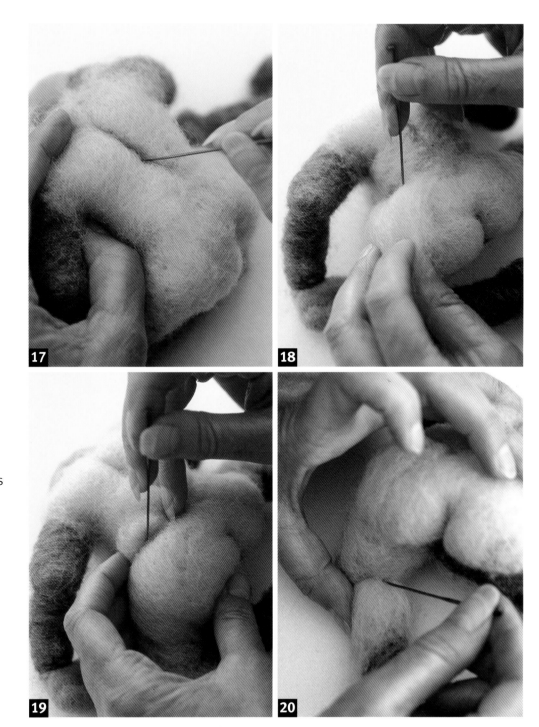

You can find many different positions when the needled figure is joined – new possibilities even present themselves during the process. A figure that crawls must, for example, have its head placed a little further back than a figure that sits. The turn of the head can also completely change the expression of a figure. The figure sitting has had its head turned a little to one side, giving it more life.

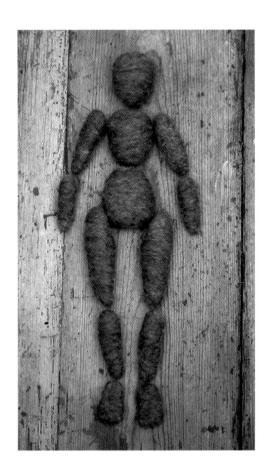

The detailed one

You can divide the body up into more basic shapes, and give each single part of the body a more detailed shape from the beginning if you want a figure with more details.

This fairytale figure has been made using detailed body shapes and long limbs, giving the opportunity of detailing the clothing.

Clothing

Since the appearance of the felting needle, clothing a figure has become much more exciting. It can be done easily and simply, but also smart and refined, adding a lot of elegant shapes. Most importantly, you can clothe the figure without hiding the shape in loose folds.

Materials
– A 40 x 40 cm foam rubber mat, at least 5 cm thick
– an ordinary felting needle (no. 1) or a silver needle (no. 2)
– carded wool in various colours

Make the clothes in a combination of colours needled directly onto the figure – and loose parts that are first needled together and then put on.

The easiest method is to needle the colour directly onto the surface in thin small amounts at a time. This enables you also to make patterns directly onto the surface. For example, striped blouse or striped socks.

Boy's clothes
The clothing is made with loose edging so that it looks as if it can be taken off.

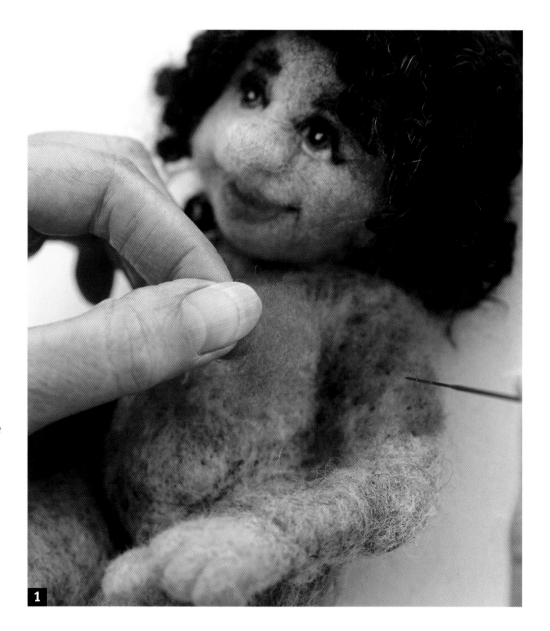

Blouse

1. For example, begin by giving the boy a blouse by needling a colour directly onto the chest of the figure.

Trousers

If the boy is to have trousers on, make loose, narrow edges for the edges of the legs and the edge at the waistband.

Place a thin piece of carded wool round the leg to measure how wide the trouser leg needs to be. After this lay the piece on the foam rubber mat. Then, firstly needle a folded edge, and afterwards needle the rest of the piece densely.

2. Place the piece round the leg again, needle it together along the side, and needle it into place along the top edge directly onto the leg.
3. Make the edge at the waistband in the same way, and needle it to the body.

The piece between the waistband edge and the bottoms of the trousers now needs to have some colour. This colour is needled on a bit at a time, so that the boy keeps his shape.

You can also make trousers that are completely unattached. Each complete side is made separately. Measure the size with a thin, loose piece of carded wool. and needle each side to the foam rubber mat with a folded edge at the top, the bottom, and the fly.

4. Lay the pieces onto the boy and needle them together on the inside of the legs and at the back. While needling you can make natural folds at the knee

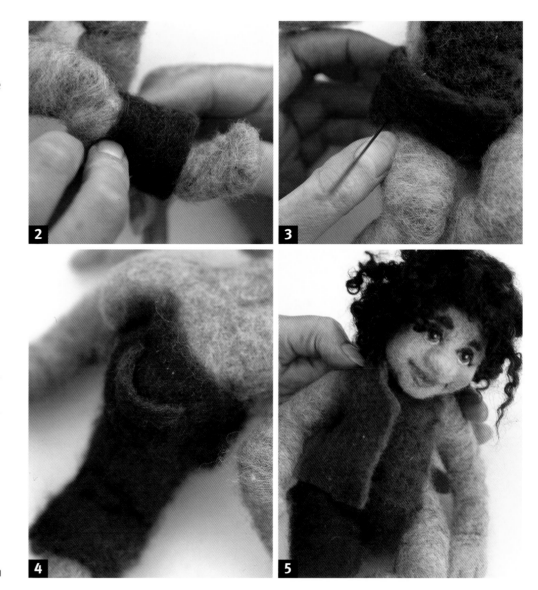

and elsewhere. Finally, you can needle on pockets. For this, needle a little piece with an edge, and let the edge of the pocket bulge out when needling it on so that it appears natural.
5. The jacket consists of two loose front

pieces that are needled to the sides of the body and around the arms up over the shoulders. The rest of the jacket is needled on using the same colour. The jacket can also be given more details, for example, a loose collar or a lapel.

Pixie clothes

1. Needle a flat piece for a hat as well as a blouse for a little pixie or gnome.

2. Place the hat round the head ...

3. ... and the blouse round the body.

4. Needle them tightly to the shapes.

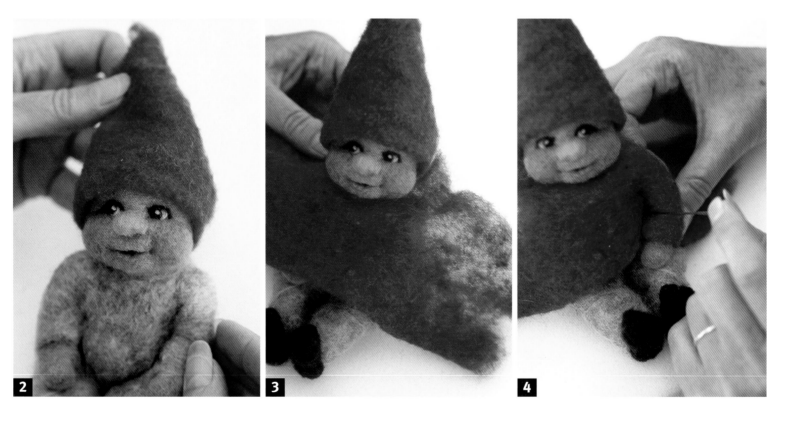

Effects and details

Staples of wool can be needled on as effects, for example, as a collar on a top, on the bottom of trouser legs, and on the edge of a hat.

Footwear

Shoes

For shoes, needle a curved piece that fits round the foot. Besides this, roll a little round shape to place under the nose of the shoe to give a natural shoe-shape. Also needle a sole in another colour (see illustrations).

1. Needle the curved piece on round the foot, with the little round shape at the toe.

2. Needle the sole on under the foot.

Boots

3. Boots are made like shoes, and afterwards a bootleg is needled around the leg.

Clogs

4. Start clogs in the same way as shoes. Then build up a point at the toe, an extra thick sole under the heel and fore-foot, and a little extra at the counter.

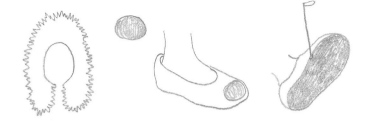

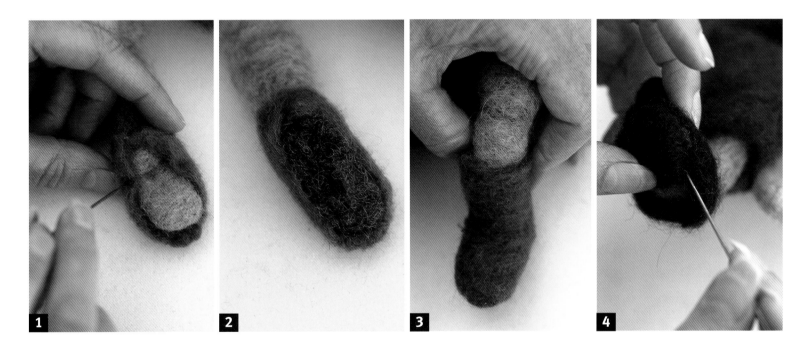

The little boy's clothing has a lot of details. He is about to lose his trousers, so his vest is showing under his blouse.

The front of the blouse is made to look as if it can be taken off. The boy has also got striped socks that are needled in a spiral up around the leg, using a thin ball of woollen string.

Here are two beings, each with their coat. The little boy wears a blouse that is needled directly to the body. In addition to this he has a loose waistcoat with staples of raw wool needled to the surface.

The little ground squirrel has got a surface of fine-fibred wool.

These figures are only about 9 cm tall, and can more or less vanish from sight in a hand. They can easily be given personality even though they are so small.

Reliefs

This technique can be used in various ways to make – complete human figures, animal figures, faces of animals and people, and landscapes.

This is a technique that is well-suited for working intuitively. For example, by beginning with a face and then using the surroundings to felt on a »story«. If you need more space than planned at first, you can easily add more carded wool as you go.

You can also combine this with sculptural felting so that three-dimensional shapes in the form of branches, arms etc. can be added. And lastly, a relief technique using raw wool as a background is an amazingly elegant, effective technique.

Face reliefs

Materials
- a 40 x 40 cm foam rubber mat, at least 5cm thick
- an ordinary felting needle (no. 1) or a silver needle (no. 2)
- a big pointed darning needle
- steel wire (1 to 1.5 mm thick)
- carded wool in one or two neutral colours, and a little coloured wool for the surface

Place a layer of carded wool that is a little thick onto the foam rubber mat, needle it lightly, leaving the edge loose. Now use the mattress technique (see page 12) to make a nice high »staple« for the face shape – the top layer of the staple should be the broadest. Fold the edge in to an oval shape while pressing out as much air as possible.

Lay the shape onto the background while still pressing out the air. Needle the shape on along the edge and into the foam rubber mat while still pressing the shape (see the photo). The firmer the shape is, the easier it is to work with.

Now follow the instructions in the section about needling a face (see pages 25 to 40).

If you wish to, you can make two faces, and have them in profile or semi-profile so that they are talking to each other.

When you make a face in profile, lay the lip over the side of the shape of the face. Apart from this the method is as described earlier.

You could lay a triangular shape on as a neck so that the face appears to come out from the background.

This relief is felted directly onto part of a fleece – the shorn off coat of a sheep – that was beautiful and curly.

The two faces are felted in semi-profile by pulling their facial expressions a little to one side of the basic shape. The leaves are needled around a shape formed of floral thread, and afterwards felted using soapy water.

Loose arm and foot

Use steel wire as a base to make a loose arm or foot to put on a relief.

Here is a description of how to make an arm. A foot is formed in basically the same way. A hand is formed using wire as shown by the illustration.

1. Cover the shape by winding wool around it. To avoid the wool slipping from your fingers, begin by putting a wad of wool around the wire as shown.
2. Twist the wad tightly …
3. … and wind the wool down over each finger.
4. Lay a flat rolled shape in the palm of the hand, fold the edge around the wire and needle it on. Lay a rolled shape on for the cushion of the thumb, and wind a layer around the palm.

It is a good idea to put a thin layer of foam rubber around the arm before covering it so that the wool does not move out of position. Use the felting needle to keep the wool in place as you are working, and, if chosen, to needle colour onto the hand and arm.

You can make nails by laying a thread of wool to mark the nail, and then filling it out with a thin finishing layer. Finally, it is good to complete the surface of the hand with a wet felting.

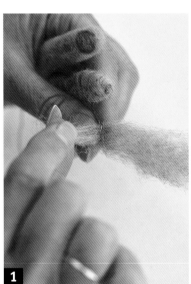

1

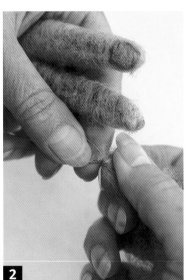

2

3

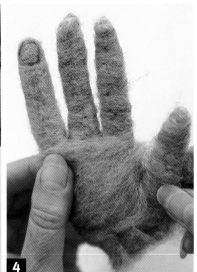

4

Background

The background the face is needled onto can be used in many different ways. You can needle a whole landscape, or you can needle a tree on the foam rubber mat beside it, and put it on so that, perhaps, its roots and branches extend beyond the frame.

Finishing and mounting is important to the work. First and foremost, you need to complete needling the surface.

For this you should use the star needle, which is the finest and the one that makes the smallest holes. The technique requires needling a little sideways (horizontally) so that you ensure a firm skin layer and each time cover a larger area than otherwise possible. Having a darning needle in your left hand can be a great help. Push this just under the surface of the skin layer, and use it to lift this layer up while needling it. This maintains the shape.

Complete needling a little area at a time. The surface must be so firm that you are able to scratch it without it »fluffing«.

If you have flat areas without relief, you can needle them using a needle holder until they feel firmly coherent.

The reverse side of the relief can be finished, by laying the face or subject on your hand and needling the back. If you want the background to be particularly strong, you can also wet felt it.

You can continue working on the background after you have finished needling the face. Here the edges are still loose and unfelted, so it is easy to add extra wool and make the picture longer and/or wider.

65

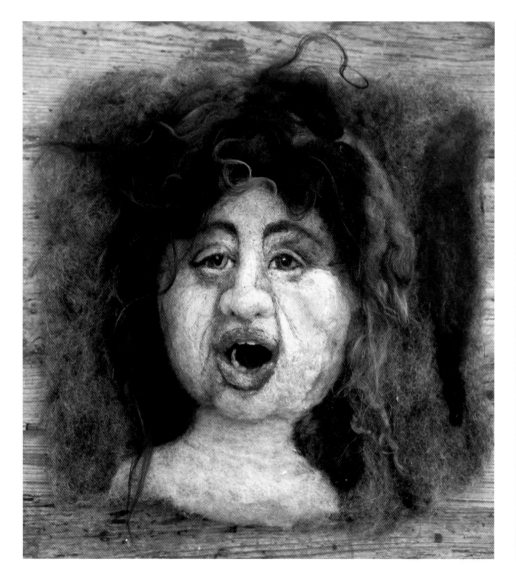

This female singer is an intensively worked face consisting of many shades and very tiny wads of surface colour, added after the shape of the face was completed. The hair has been chosen to emphasise the facial colours and the woman's temperament. This relief could be extended – perhaps by adding a long body beneath.

It might be tempting to needle a loose felt hand onto the picture of this cunning young witch. Another possibility is to give the girl a tattered dress.

In this case I wanted to achieve a frail, poetic expression, and therefore chose a white coarse-fibred wool that looks quite like porcelain.

For this relief the background was first wet felted with a flat face. Then a relief face was needled on, after the background had been washed and was once again dry.

A relief needled directly onto a felted fleece. Here you see examples of
faces in both profile and partly profile. For full-profile faces, avoid needling
one side of the basic shape to the background so that you are able to lay
the facial expressions round the edge.

Here you can see a big relief, which has a combination of a flat needled background and a felted piece of raw wool. The characters in the picture are interacting together, so that they are aware of one another. This is due to their facial expressions and the way the faces are turned.

This flat man-sized figure has also got a coloured back, so that it can hang in the middle of a room and revolve.

The way the shading has been applied and the figure built up make it appear three-dimensional.

Like the previous photos this is also a flat needled man-sized figure with a coloured back.

If these two figures are hung in the middle of a room, it looks as if they stand talking to each other.

Croquis-relief

You can get a whole human figure on a croquis-relief.

Materials

- a 40 x 40 cm foam rubber mat, at least 5 cm thick
- an ordinary felting needle (no. 1) or a silver needle (no. 2)
- carded wool for the background and subject
- a 5-needle holder
- equipment for wet felting (optional)

Needle or wet felt a background of suitable size. You can choose to use natural-coloured and very coarse wool to make the subject – this can give a very elegant result. In fact, it is possible just to tease the washed wool or card it roughly if you use the right coarse types of wool. Here it is helpful to use a needle holder with a number of needles.

Choose to work from memory or use a sketch as a model. The two techniques used most are the rolling technique and the mattress one (see pages 10, 11 and 12). Use the wool to needle a faint outline to get the proportions right.

After this, begin by building up layers where the figure juts out. For example, make a »pile of mattresses« and lay them on as hip and thigh. If required, lay on a flat rolled shape with loose ends as the stomach. The breasts are also rolled shapes with loose ends. Remember that it is not necessary for you to cover all of the background firmly when you have started with a sketch.

Now continue by building small amounts onto others, and needling them into shape until the figure is finished. You can simplify things so much that the face is just a shape (or not even that) – the same is true of the hands.

The croquis-relief is made on a background of very coarse needled wool. A more fine-fibred wool is used for the actual subject to emphasise the shapes of the bodies. It is also possible to continue working on a relief, developing the shapes further.

The inspiration for making the orang-utans has come from a piece of coloured raw fleece of wool in exactly the right nuance matching an ape. Notice the wrinkles that are made by rolling the wool around a straw.

Raw wool felting

Materials
- a 40 x 40 cm foam rubber mat, at least 5 cm thick
- an ordinary felting needle (no. 1) or a silver needle (no. 2)
- raw wool

If you are fortunate enough to have a fleece that is felted – or partially felted – at the base, but which still retains an attractive surface, you can needle a subject directly into the fleece. If it does not hang together completely, needle a thin piece of carded wool onto the foam rubber mat, and then lay the fleece on top. Needle the fleece onto the carded wool by needling between the staples while holding up the tips.

The raw wool is now ready. Spread the staples out to the sides a little where the subject is to be, and then needle directly down into the raw wool.

For example, the subject could be a lion with a mane, faces of trolls in a wood, or something completely different.

A real find – a completely perfect piece of felted fleece!! Just the right natural colour for a relief of a lion, where there has also been room for one of the lions raised front paws and a faint-hearted little lion cub.

Hedgehog faces with small pointed snouts are quite simple. The quills are made from a wad of raw wool.

The face of the lion is a little more detailed, with details on its nose and its slanting eyes.

A cylinder-shaped snout and two or three double chins is characteristic of a pig.

Animal faces

If you are going to make an animal face, it is often an advantage, in relation to an understanding of proportions, to have one or more photos of the animal.

Many of the techniques for making animal and human faces are common. The most important thing is to learn to divide the animal's face up into shapes. Look first at the basic shape, which is always some kind of circle (ball). Then look for the shape of the nose, which can be divided up further for some animals.

Basic shapes for different animals are shown below. The nose/snout is shown in profile under each of them.

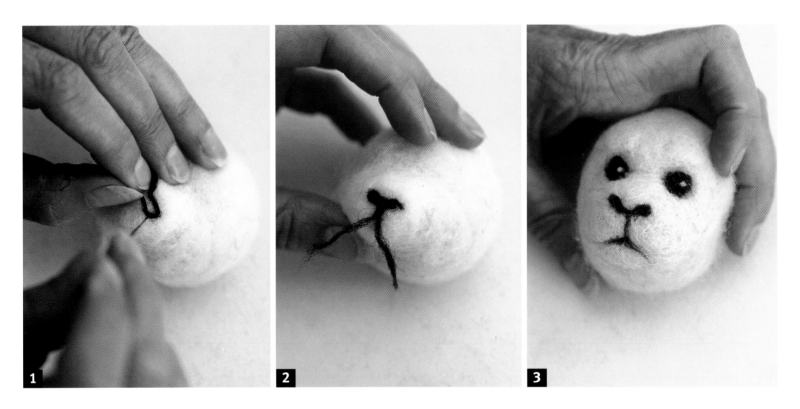

A couple of easy animal faces

A baby seal and a monkey are shown here as examples of a couple of easy animal faces.

Materials
- a 40 x 40 cm foam rubber mat, at least 5 cm thick
- an ordinary felting needle (no. 1) or a silver needle (no. 2)
- carded wool in a neutral colour for the basic shape, a little colour for the surface (white for the seal, medium brown for the monkey, and black and white for the eyes)

Baby seal

1. Roll and needle a big white ball for the head, and a little flat oval one for the snout. Needle the snout onto the head. Roll a very thin thread, pulling it out of the black wool. Shape the nose, as shown, and needle it.

2. Needle from the nose downward to the corners of the mouth. Needle this very firmly.

3. Roll two black circles for the eyes, and needle them. Roll a little tiny white spot and needle it into the black eye. If you choose, a thin yellow stripe can be needled on the black edge.

Finally, use a darning needle to pull the wool out a little for the upper lip shapes and over the eyes.

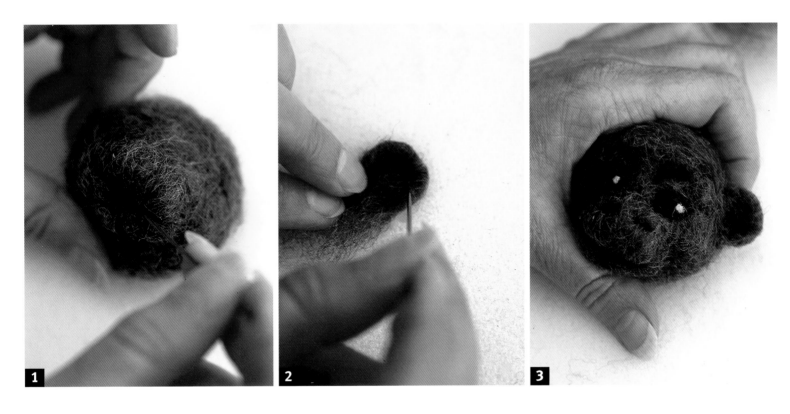

Monkey

1. Roll and needle a big brown ball for the head, and a smaller brown ball for the lower face. Needle the lower face to the head. Shape a groove for the mouth by needling deeply a number of times. Roll a thin black sausage, and needle it into the groove.

2. Shape and needle two ears, and needle them on.

3. Roll two black circles for the eyes, and needle them. Roll a little white spot and needle it into the eye. Then make two holes for the nostrils by needling a lot of times. Needle a little black into the nostrils. Finally, give the monkey eyebrows by needling two narrow black stripes above the eyes.

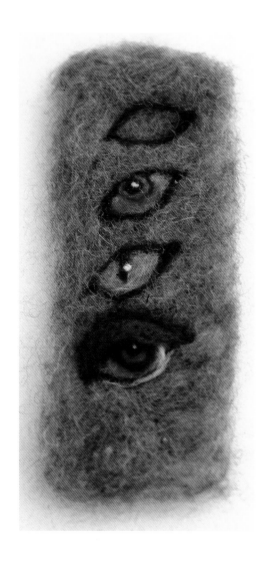

Some common animal features

The round basic shape with attached nose-shape/snout is one of the common features of animals.

Looking at animal snouts, they are variations of the shape shown to the right. The shape is made, by rolling the dark wool round a straw, pulling it off, and needling it on in the shape appropriate to the chosen animal.

On animals, the outer corner of the eye is nearly always higher than the inner one – i.e. the eye is always a bit slanting. It often gives a good effect to make a loose arched eyelid for some animals – as explained and shown on page 34. You can achieve an excellent effect by putting a light stripe under the eye, getting it to look as if the eye is wet.

Nearly every animal ears begin like a »pipe« at the base, widening out upwards. Therefore, needle a flat shape and gather it as you put it on (see the illustration in the lower right corner).

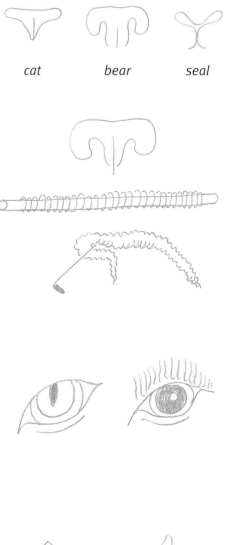

cat   bear   seal

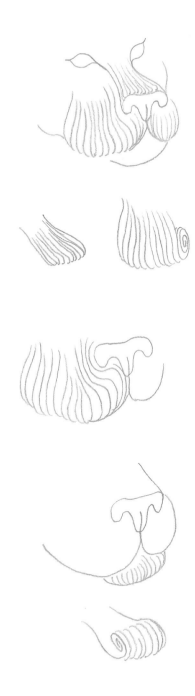

Many animal noses have a distinctly marked bridge that can be made by rolling a narrow shape with a loose end, as explained in the rolling technique on pages 10 and 11. The shape is needled on top of the shape for the snout.

A number of animals have also got a bipartite upper lip. You can make this by rolling a wide shape with a loose end (see rolling technique on pages 10 and 11). Needle the shape onto both sides of the nose while laying and shaping it in along the edge of the nose.

The lower lip is an independent shape. Roll it in the same way as a loose-ended piece (see rolling technique on pages 10 and 11), and needle it to the underside of the bipartite upper lip.

Some animal faces have characteristic shapes that make them distinctive. For example, many of them have a round arched shape above the eye. Also make this shape using the rolling technique, and needle it on with the loose end up.

All in all, the rolling technique can nearly always be used if you need to make a shape more marked – a broader or higher cheekbone, a more arched forehead etc.

A thin finishing layer can be used to cover a rolled edge if it is too noticeable.

bear

lion

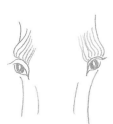

horse

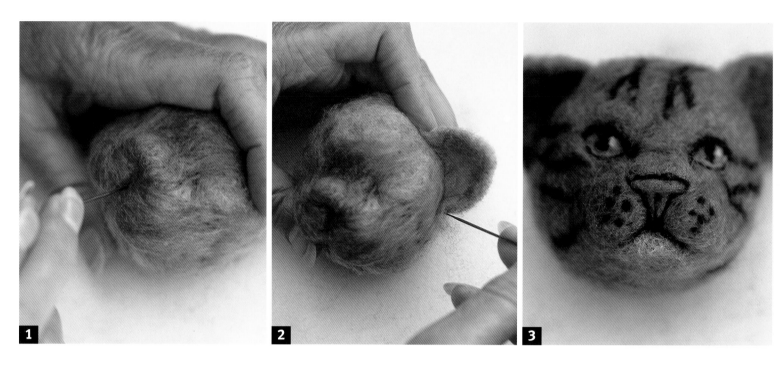

A couple of detailed animal faces

Here are examples of a couple of more detailed animal faces.

Cat

Materials
– a 40 x 40 cm foam rubber mat, at least 5 cm thick
– an ordinary felting needle (no. 1) or a silver needle (no. 2)
– a thin straw
– carded wool in cat colours

1. Roll and needle a large ball for the head, and a little flat cylindrical one for the nose. Lay a thin finishing layer around the joint. Roll a flat bridge of the nose, as explained in the rolling technique on pages 10 and 11, and needle it on.

2. Lay a flat shape up as the ear, fold in the edge and needle it. Needle the ear on while shaping it. Shape a second ear in the same way.

3. Roll some pink wool around the straw for the snout, and shape it while needling it onto the end of the shape for the nose. Roll a shape for the bipartite upper lip, and needle it on. After this roll a shape for the lower lip. Roll a very thin dark brown thread for the contour of the eye. Needle this contour for the slanting eye on – allowing the line to continue into the corner of the eye. Fill the eye out with a yellow/green colour. Add on a black line down through the eye for the pupil. Needle on a little white spot. Needle stripes on the cat, if you wish.

Here you see two faces with common fundamental features that nevertheless become very different in the process. Especially the shapes and lengths of the nose and the ears make the difference.

Notice the white stripe along the bottom edge of the cat's eye, giving it the »wet« look.

Lion

The lion is felted as a relief here, but you can use the same instruction for a round head.

Materials
- a 40 x 40 cm foam rubber mat, at least 5 cm thick
- an ordinary felting needle (no. 1) or a silver needle (no. 2)
- a thin straw
- carded wool in lion colours
- raw wool

Prepare a piece of raw wool as described on page 75.

The basic shape of the head has here been made using natural colour, and lion colour has been used on the surface.

Special attention has been paid to the colours of the eyes and the delicate play of colour on the surface of this lion portrait. Colours have been found to match the excellent natural colours of the mane.

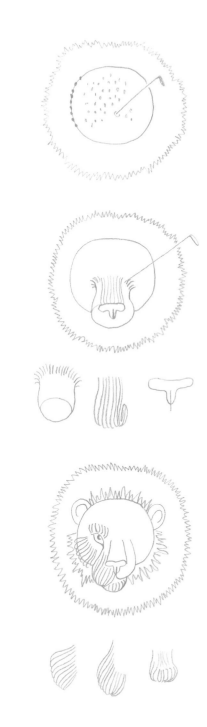

Make a flat round basic shape and needle it into the piece of raw wool, as described in the relief technique, so that the air is pressed out of the wool. Needle the surface.

Roll and needle a cylindrical shape for the nose. Needle it onto the shape for the head, put a finishing layer over the joint and needle it. Roll a shape for the bridge of the nose, using the rolling technique (see the illustration) and needle it on.

Roll dark brown wool around the straw, and shape it into a snout, while placing it at the end of the bridge of the nose.

Roll two shapes for the bipartite upper lip, and needle each of them on. After this, roll a shape for the lower lip/the chin and needle it on.

Needle the eyes, as explained for the cat on page 82. Also roll an arched shape and needle it above the eye so that it forms a bulge. Needle the ears, as explained for the cat. More details can be done, as shown in the picture on the previous page, if you wish.

Fix a little of the raw wool from the background piece onto the forehead and the cheeks.

Animals with bodies

Just as there are similarities when building up animals' faces, so there are when building up their bodies. And once you have grasped the way you can divide up the animal's body, it is not difficult to get the animal to look as it *should* look.

If we look at an animal we are familiar with, a dog, we can look at the body and the legs as three separate parts:

- A body shape that is rectangular and most often broadest at the front where the ribcage is.
- The front legs that are almost the same width the whole way up.

- The hind legs that get broader the nearer they get to the top, and which have a clearly marked backward »elbow«.

If we also study other animals for these shapes we often find the same common features. So once you have made an animal, other animals are just variations with slightly different shaped legs, and perhaps a body that is a little longer.

As you are working it is possible to give the animal different positions, so that it sits, lies or turns its body. In order to do this, do not roll the shape for the body too firmly.

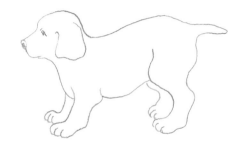

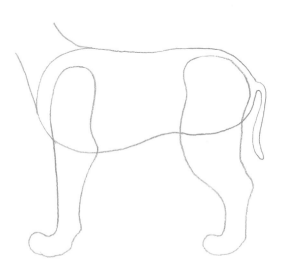

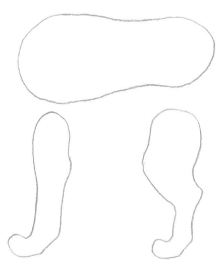

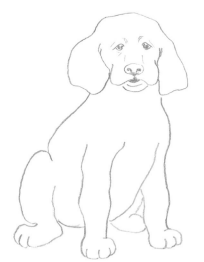

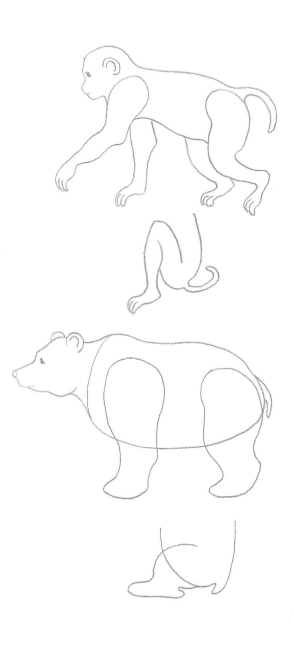

- Begin by looking closely at the animal you wish to needle, and find out what the actual shape of the body is.
- Also notice what the line of the back is like, and how far down the elbow is on the hind legs. This can be very different – for example, the elbow of a bear and a lion is fairly low.
- Also take note of how thick the legs are in relation to the body, and how big a gap there is between front and hind legs.

The easiest is to start making animals very small, see the little bear cub on page 92, for example.

  After felting your first animal, your second one will be much easier to do.

Dog

The dog shown here is approx. 20 cm long and 14 cm high.

Materials
- a 40 x 40 cm foam rubber mat, at least 5 cm thick
- an ordinary felting needle (no. 1) or a siver needle (no. 2)
- a big sharp-pointed darning needle
- a thin straw
- carded wool in dog colours
- raw wool (optional)
- a photo or illustration of a dog

Roll and needle a shape for the body, see the illustration on page 86. Roll it firmly, but not so firm that it cannot be bent a little – allowing you to give the animal different positions.

Roll the hind legs – rolling extra wool for the top part so that the shape for the thigh becomes flat and not round. Stick a darning needle in where the elbow for the hind leg is to be, and pull it back. Needle on a little extra just above the elbow so that the leg curves.

Roll the front legs. Also push the darning needle in here where the elbow is to be, and pull it back.

1. Needle the legs onto the body by needling along the edges.

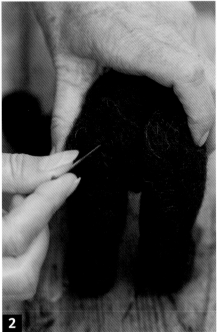

2. Position the hind legs so that they meet at the back of the dog. Needle a thin finishing layer over all of the joints.

3. Needle a tail by rolling wool tightly round the straw – so that the tail is thicker at one end. Take the wool off the straw, and needle the tail together. Spread the fibres at the thick end, and roll the other end into a point with your fingers (or wet felt it). Needle on the tail.

4. Roll a shape for the neck and needle it on.

5. Needle the dog's head, using the same method as the one explained for the cat, see page 82. The ears can hang or be pointed. Needle on the head, and cover the joint with a finishing layer.

The eyes are a round shape in a dark colour. Needle a thin white or golden stripe on along the bottom edge of the eye. Finally, needle a very tiny white spot into the dark shape.

It may be necessary to needle on extra wool in some places, and in others to hollow the shape by needling a lot.

Finally, »dress« the dog by covering it all over with raw wool, needling it on a little at a time.

Needle spaces between the claws on the paws.

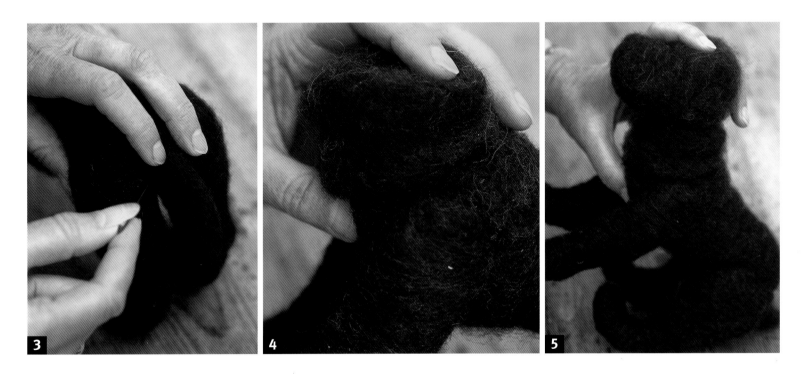

Sitting bear

The bear shown here is approx. 25 cm high and 15 cm wide. I have chosen brown wool with light tips for the bear in order to achieve a good furry effect. This wool has not been carded, only teased a little while I am working on it.

You can also needle a bear from carded wool, and then needle a layer of raw wool onto the surface.

Materials
– a 40 x 40 cm foam rubber mat, at least 5 cm thick
– an ordinary felting needle (no. 1) or a silver needle (no. 2)
– a thin straw
– carded wool and raw wool in bear colours
– a photo or illustration of a bear

A mother bear with cubs. Felting a little family unit is enjoyable. The cubs have been made very small and playful, and mother bear given a worried look.

First, roll and needle a shape for the body. Then needle the legs – note that thighs of a bear are very long, their lower legs very short, and their paws very flat, see the illustration.

Place the legs on the body, so that they meet at the back, and needle them on along the edge. Needle a finishing layer over the joints.

Needle a short neck and fix it on. Needle the head as explained for the cat on page 82. A bear's nose is long and narrow, and it's snout is characteristic – sticking out a lot and having loose wings. The eyes are round, small, and black, and close to the nose.

Put a little golden stripe below each eye. Roll a very tiny white spot, and needle it into the black part. Make the ears by taking a good wad of wool and rolling the edge in to round it. Needle them, and place them quite far back on the head. Attach the head, trying possible different positions. There may now be a need for more shape in different places. For example for the stomach and hindquarters, and perhaps the flanks. Use the rolling technique (see pages 10 and 11) for the stomach, and the mattress technique (see page 12) for the other shapes.

Make the claws round the straw by rolling a little bit of black wool on at one end and pulling it off. Roll the point well between your fingers, roll a little of the base-coloured wool round the bottom part, and needle the claws on under the paw.

When all of the claws have be attached, cover with a finishing layer, and then needle on the pads. Finish off by needling on a little stumpy tail.

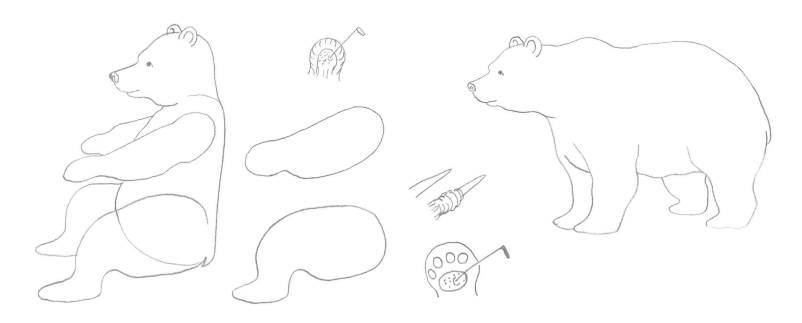

Bear cub

The bear is approx. 10 cm high and 15 cm wide.

The bear cub is easy to make and vary, so that you can soon have a small litter of young cubs in different positions. The fact that the bear is so small makes it much easier to control the shape.

Make all the parts a little soft so that you can bend and shape them.

Materials
- a 40 x 40 cm foam rubber mat, at least 5 cm thick
- an ordinary felting needle (no. 1) or a silver needle (no. 2)
- a thin straw
- carded wool and raw wool in bear colours
- a photo or illustration of a bear

Roll a body shape with »sway« in it, and small thick front and hind legs, see the illustration. Needle on the legs, imagining that the bear is tumbling about playing. Needle small paws, and attach them to the hind legs. Cover the joints with a thin layer of wool. For the front legs, it is sufficient just to needle the bottom end a little flat and needle on small pads.

Needle a little round ball for the head, and a smaller round one for the nose/snout. Needle this onto the head, and cover it with a thin finishing layer at the joint. Roll just a bit of black wool round the straw, and needle it on as the snout.

Roll two small black balls for the eyes, and needle them on close to the edge of the nose. Needle a very thin white stripe along each of the brown bear cubs' eyeballs.

Roll a little round, flat shape for the ears, and needle them on. Possibly, try turning the head in relation to the body before needling it on. Then needle it on, and, if necessary, give the joint finishing layer.

When you have joined the little bear together, you can bend and turn the legs to give it the best and funniest shape. Needle it, so that the bear keeps this shape. Finally, needle on a little stumpy tail.

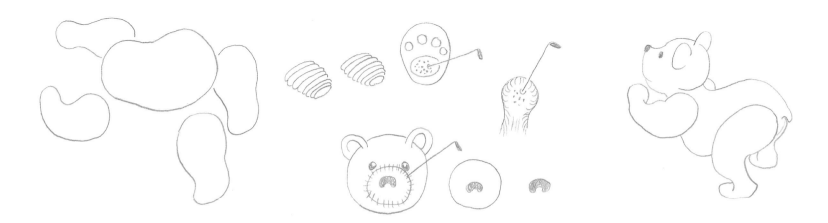

The polar bear has a more torpedo-shaped body than the brown bear, enabling it to »shoot« through the water. Its legs appear thicker and shorter, and its face is flatter, with a slight curve on the upper side of the nose. In this way, you can analyse the body and what makes it different from other animals, before you start needling.

Coarse white wool is used for the polar bear. This needs to be needled a lot before the surface is firm enough.

Theatre figures

Many of the techniques that have been described in this book are suitable for making theatre puppets. This section shows examples of how you can adapt them to various models.

Easy theatre figure

Small heads of both animals and people can be used extremely simply.

1. Densely needle a flat piece of carded wool – possibly using a 5-needle holder. Arrange the piece under the head, and needle it on underneath.
2. Needle a small felted hand (or two) into the edge by folding it around the hand like a sleeve.

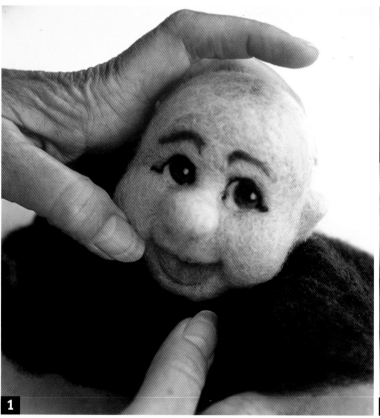

A couple of small slyboots out to play tricks! Or perhaps they are two
sweet, happy pixies?

These figures can sit decoratively on the back of a sofa. But you can also
have a lot of fun animating them while telling a story. They come
immediately to life if you put them on your arm, hold their hands, and move
them.

Finger puppet

A finger puppet is a charming, effective little figure. Put it on your finger, and pull the sleeve of your blouse up over your hand. There it sits, looking over the edge.

1. Needle a flat piece the size of your finger. Needle a small head, and needle a little neck onto it.
2. Pack the body piece round the neck, and needle this on.
3. Needle the little, hollow body shape carefully together so that it fits the finger closely. To avoid pricking your finger needle sideways.

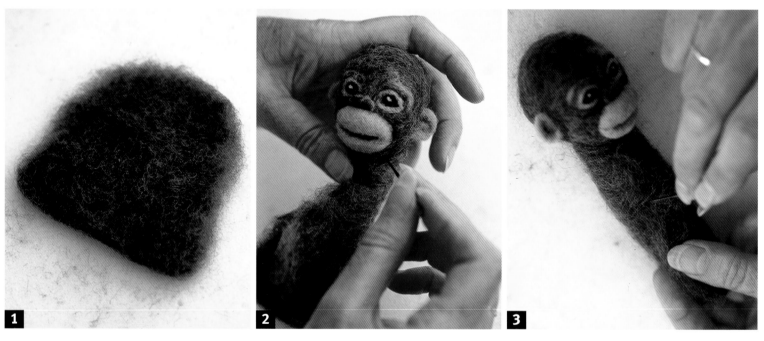

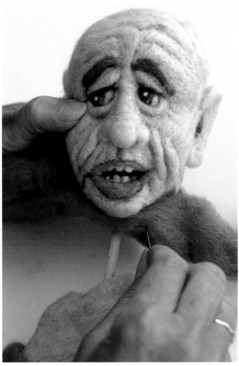

Figures on sticks

A stick figure is a much-loved theatre figure. It can be constructed very simply and yet have a big effect.

Needle a head with a face. Bore a hole under the neck using your scissors, and stick a bamboo cane up into the hole. Needle a long roll for the arms, and attach the middle of it under the head. Felt the hands on some wire (see page 64), and needle them onto the ends of the arms. Nail flower canes onto the hands by holding the end of the cane under the palm of the hand and hammering the nail through the hand into the cane.

Figure with one arm

For this, a thick, wet-felted rope is joined to a head so that
the rope becomes both body and arm.

Start by needling a head with a face. Wet-felt the rope on a
mat of straw by making a thick roll of wool with a tuft of raw
wool put into one of the ends. The end without the tuft must
be kept dry and off the mat when the roll is made wet using
soapy water. The rest is rolled in the mat until it is well felted.
Swill the roll, and let it dry. Spread the loose end and needle
the head securely onto it.

Witch with a loose arm made on wire base

The witch's head has got a needled neck that you hold in your right hand, while also holding the witch's long arm. Use your left hand to move the witch's hand. The arm is shaped as explained on page 64.

Simple and effective.

Head with arms needled directly onto it

This figure has no body. It can be placed in lots of amusing ways, and is surprisingly lifelike when animated just by moving its arms slightly.

These are a couple of »story figures« that in a way are more lively thanks to their lack of lower body. It is easy to convince yourself that they pop up over the edge of something and look at you, ready to tell a tale. You can also place them in the palm of your hand or on your shoulder.

Large figure with pipe cleaner skeleton

This figure is very movable, and has got the advantage of being able to be made the size of a human being. The figure is built onto a skeleton made out of long pipe cleaners. These are easy to put together by winding them round each other, and easy to get the wool to bind to.

Materials
- an ordinary felting needle (no. 1) or a silver needle (no. 2)
- wire (1.5 to 2 mm thick)
- carded wool in different colours
- raw wool for the hair
- long pipe cleaners

Shape a skeleton as shown to the left in the illustration. Wind wool round the skeleton to make a suitable base. You can use coarse wool and waste wool for the very middle. Use the felting needle as a help, but do not needle so much that the figure becomes stiff.

After doing this add extra shapes to the surface. Fingers and toes with wire skeletons could be made as described in relief felting, see page 64.

Roll an oval ball for the head. Press it into the ring, and cover it with a finishing layer. You may choose to make an opening in the back to make it easier to operate the puppet, see the illustration at the right.

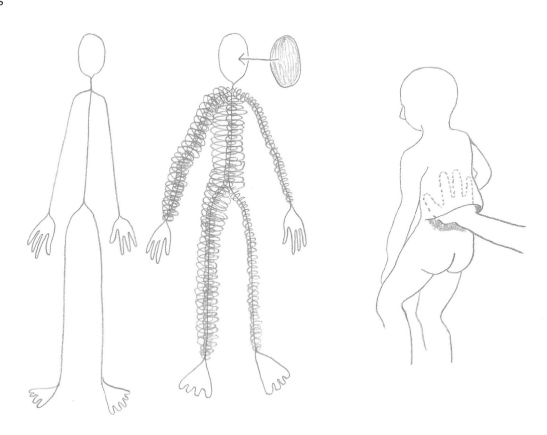

Rasmus the Troll is just as big as a three or four year-old child, and he also looks nearly as alive because he is soft with movable parts.

The figure is made out of very coarse wool, needled onto a pipe cleaner skeleton. His face can – depending on the circumstances – look both happy and sad.

List of suppliers

Ateliers Camelot
Amacre Drive
Hooe, Plymouth PL9 9RJ
UK
Tel. +44 (0)1752 403321
www.ateliers.demon.co.uk
– *Carded wool, felting accessories and books on felting.*

Ashford Handicrafts Ltd
415 West Street
P O Box 474
Ashburton
New Zealand
Tel: +64 3 308 9087
www.ashford.co.nz
– *Carded wool, books on felting.*

Birgitte Krag Hansen
Bjergmarken 50 st. th.
4300 Holbæk
Denmark
Tel. +45 5943 9316
www.feltmaking.dk
– *Felting needles and needle holders with two, five, and ten needles.*

Filzrausch
Frieder Glatzer
Hagenweg 2b
37081 Göttingen
Germany
Tel. +49 0551 67515
www.filzrausch.de
– *Felting accessories, carded wool and books on felting.*

Harrisville Designs
Center Village
Box 806
Harrisville
New Hampshire
03450 USA.
Tel. +1 800 338 9415 or +1 603 827 3333
www.harrisville.com
– *Carded wool in specially beautiful mixtures – 30 to 40 different shades.*

Henrichsens Uldspinderi
Christiansgade 7
7800 Skive
Denmark
Tel. +45 9752 0630
www.henrichsens-uldspinderi.dk
– *Carded wool in mixed natural colours and dyed (especially suitable for sculptural felting).*

Hillesvåg Ullvarefabrikk
N-5915 Hjelmås
Norway
Tel. +47 5635 7800
www.ull.no
– *Coloured carded wool and coloured raw wool.*

Kartehuset
Ulla Winding
Vesterskovvej 8
5792 Aarslev
Denmark
Tel. +45 6599 1919
www.kartehuset.dk
– *Felting accessories. Needlefelt, thin materials, lanasyn colours, and books on felting.*

Seehawer & Siebert
Heuberger Hof 1
72108 Rottenburg a.N.
Germany
Tel. +49 7472 3019
www.naturfasern.com
– *Coloured carded wool.*

Spektrum
Kirsten Lundbergh
Fredensvej 48
2920 Charlottenlund
Denmark
Tel. +45 3962 8500
– *Colours for dyeing wool.*

Susan's Fiber Shop
N250 Hwy.A
Columbus
Wi 53925
USA
Tel. +1 (920) 623-4237
www.susansfibershop.com
– *Carded wool, all kinds of special*
effect material and books on felting.

The Fiber Studio
P.O. Box 637
Henniker,
New Hampshire 03242-0637
USA
Tel. +1 (603)428-7830
www.fiberstudio.com
– *Carded wool, all kinds of special*
effect material and books on felting.

Walter Vetsch Wollspinnerei
7231 Pragg-Jenaz
Schweiz
Tel. +41 081 332 13 72
– *Coloured carded wool.*

Åddebo Ull
Nektarvägen 31
810 65 Skärplinge
Sweden
Tel. +46 0294 30020
www.addeboull.com
– *Natural and dyed carded Finn wool*
and books on felting.

Associations

GRIMA, Danish felting association,
Publishes a membership magazine,
organises courses etc.
www.grima.dk

International Feltmakers Association
Publishes a magazine.
www.feltmakers.com

National Association of Danish Sheep-
breeding
Arranges contact to sheep farmers, and
organises sheep days.
www.sheep.dk

North American Felters' Network
Publishes a newsletter including,
among other things, lists of courses
and exhibitions throughout the world.
Free »mailing list« on felting.
www.peak.org/~spark/feltmakers.html

Word list

Carding. Combing wool so that the fibres lie parallel.

Carded wool (Batts). Wool that has been carded on a machine – usually in broad lengths.

Card/Carding brush. A hand tool for carding (combing) wool.

Carding drum. A carding machine with two drums worked manually using a handle.

Fibre. Hair – in this case from a sheep.

Finishing layer. A thin piece of carded wool that is laid over for hiding or binding together.

Mix. Mixing/blending colours and fibres.

Net. A plastic fly net for laying over a surface, to keep it in place when wet-felting.

Raw wool. Unprocessed wool, straight from the sheep.

Staple. A portion of wool that together forms a bunch from a fleece of a sheep.

Teasing. Loosening wool by pulling it apart.

Tops. Thin lengths of carded wool.

Booklist

Charlotte Buch
Arbejdshæfte til beklædningsfilt (Workbook on Clothing Felt)
Hvalsø, 1999

Mary E. Burkett
The art of the felt maker
Abbot Hall Art Gallery, 1979

Anette Damgaard
Filt: kunst, teknik, historie (Felt: art, technique, history)
Hovedland, 1994

Monika und Jürgen Fergg
Filz und Form (Felt and Form)
Verlag Paul Haupt, 1999

Ida Hamre
Marionet og Menneske: animations-teater, billedteater (Puppet and Person: animation theatre, picture theatre)
Drama, 1997

Birgitte Krag Hansen
Filt i form (Felt in Shape)
Høst, 1992

Birgitte Krag Hansen
Skulpturel filtning (Sculptural Felting)
Høst, 1999

May Jacobsen Hvistendahl
Håndlaget filt (Handmade Felt)
Cappelen, 2000

Marlene Lang
Filzkunst: Tradition und Experiment (The Art of Felt: Tradition and Experiment)
Verlag Paul Haupt, 2001

Gunilla Paetau Sjöberg
Tova: gammal teknik på nytt sätt (Felt: Old Technique in New Style)
LTs Förlag, 1996

Ayala Talpai
The Felting Needle from Factory to Fantasy
Diligence Woodwork & Design, 2000

Anne Einset Vickrey
Needle Felting: art techniques and projects
Craft Works Pub., 2002

Index